Real World Search & Seizure

A Street Handbook for Law Enforcement

MATTHEW J. MEDINA

Looseleaf Law Publications, Inc.

43-08 162nd Street
Flushing, NY 11358
www.LooseleafLaw.com
800-647-5547

Library of Congress Cataloging-In-Publication Data

Medina, Matthew.
    Real world search & seizure : a street handbook for law enforcement / Matthew Medina.
        p. cm.
    Includes index.
    ISBN 1-932777-31-8
    1. Searches and seizures--United States. I. Title. II. Title: Real world search and seizure.
    KF9630.M43 2006
    345.73'0522--dc22

                                                    2006012608

13 digit ISBN: 978-1-932777-31-4

Cover design by *Sans Serif, Inc.* Saline, Michigan

Make Your Arrest *Stick!*

An Invaluable Guide to Legal and Effective Searches and Seizures For:

- *Patrol Officers*
- *Community Service Officers*
- Community Policing Officers
- *Deputy Sheriffs*
- *Detectives*
- *Prosecutors*
- *Criminal Defense Lawyers*
- *Law Students*
- *Criminal Justice Students*
- *Public Safety Officers*
- *Security Specialists*
- *Correctional Officers*
- *Parole Officers*
- *Probation Officers*
- *School Liaisons*
- *Anyone interested in the Real World of Search and Seizure*

Table of Contents

About the Author v

Introduction vii

Part I
WARRANTLESS SEARCHES AND SEIZURES 1

Chapter 1
Police Search & Seizure of Property 3
    1.1   WHEN DOES THE FOURTH AMENDMENT APPLY
           AND WHY DOES IT MATTER? 3
    1.2   WHEN DOES THE FOURTH AMENDMENT *NOT*
           APPLY? 5
    1.3   WHAT CONSTITUTES ABANDONED PROPERTY? . . 6
    1.4   WHAT IS A SEARCH? 8
    1.5   WHAT CONSTITUTES A SEIZURE OF PROPERTY? 10

Chapter 2
Preliminary Investigation:
Stopping & Questioning People 13
    2.1   WHAT ARE THE THREE TYPES OF POLICE-
           CITIZEN CONTACT? 14
    2.2   WHAT CONSTITUTES A CONSENSUAL POLICE
           ENCOUNTER? 15
    2.3   WHAT IS A *TERRY* STOP? 17
    2.4   WHAT IS *REASONABLE SUSPICION*? 19
    2.5   WHAT JUSTIFICATION IS NEEDED TO CONDUCT
           A BRIEF PAT DOWN SEARCH OF A SUSPECT FOR
           WEAPONS? 21
    2.6   WHEN DOES A *TERRY* STOP BECOME AN
           ARREST AND WHY DOES IT MATTER? 23

Chapter 3
Arresting Suspects 25
    3.1   WHAT CONSTITUTES AN *ARREST* AND WHAT
           JUSTIFICATION DO POLICE NEED TO MAKE A
           WARRANTLESS PUBLIC ARREST? 26

3.2   WHEN IS IT PERMISSIBLE FOR POLICE TO ARREST A SUSPECT WITHOUT A WARRANT? ... 27

3.3   WHAT IS *PROBABLE CAUSE* IN THE CONTEXT OF AN ARREST? 28

3.4   WHEN DO POLICE NEED *PROBABLE CAUSE* TO CONTINUE THEIR DETENTION OF A SUSPECT? . 29

3.5   WHAT INFORMATION CAN POLICE USE AS A BASIS FOR *PROBABLE CAUSE* TO ARREST A SUSPECT? 30

3.6   MAY *PROBABLE CAUSE* BE DERIVED FROM AN *ANONYMOUS TIP?* 31

3.7   WHAT IS A *SEARCH INCIDENT TO ARREST?* ... 32

Chapter 4

Search, Seizure and Arrest of Suspects in Vehicles 35

4.1   WHAT JUSTIFICATION DO POLICE NEED TO STOP A VEHICLE? 35

4.2   WHEN IS IT PERMISSIBLE FOR POLICE TO SEARCH A VEHICLE WITHOUT A WARRANT? ... 36

4.3   WHEN IS IT PERMISSIBLE FOR POLICE TO SEARCH THE *PASSENGERS OF A VEHICLE?* 38

4.4   WHAT IS AN INVENTORY SEARCH? 39

Chapter 5

Suspects and House Searches 41

5.1   UNDER WHAT CIRCUMSTANCES MAY POLICE SEARCH A SUSPECT'S HOME? 41

5.2   WHAT ARE *EXIGENT CIRCUMSTANCES* THAT WOULD JUSTIFY A WARRANTLESS ENTRY INTO A HOME? 42

5.3   MAY POLICE ARREST A SUSPECT IN HIS OWN HOME WITHOUT A WARRANT? 43

5.4   DO POLICE NEED A WARRANT TO ARREST A *SUSPECT* IN A THIRD-PARTY'S HOME? 44

5.5   MAY POLICE SEARCH PEOPLE *NOT THE SUBJECT OF A WARRANT* THAT HAPPEN TO BE PRESENT DURING ITS EXECUTION? 45

5.6   MAY A *THIRD-PARTY CONSENT* TO THE SEARCH OF A PERSON'S *HOME?* 46

Chapter 6
Consent Searches 49
    6.1   WHAT IS A CONSENT SEARCH? 49
    6.2   ARE POLICE *REQUIRED* TO TELL A SUSPECT
           THAT THEY HAVE A RIGHT TO REFUSE TO GIVE
           CONSENT? 51
    6.3   MAY A *THIRD-PARTY* GIVE POLICE CONSENT
           TO SEARCH ANOTHER PERSON'S PROPERTY? . . 52
    6.4   MAY PARENTS CONSENT TO THE SEARCH OF
           THEIR CHILDREN'S PROPERTY? 52
    6.5   WHAT ARE THE *LIMITS* OF A CONSENT SEARCH? 53
    Police Checklists 54

Part II
WARRANTS 61

Chapter 7 63
Searches and Seizures Requiring Warrants 63
    7.1   WHAT IS A WARRANT AND WHEN DO POLICE
           NEED TO OBTAIN ONE? 64
    7.2   WHO MAY ISSUE A WARRANT? 65
    7.3   WHAT ARE THE GENERAL REQUIREMENTS OF A
           VALID WARRANT? 66
    7.4   ARE THERE ANY SPECIAL RULES REGARDING
           THE EXECUTION OF A WARRANT? 67
    7.5   MAY A WARRANT BE EXECUTED AT THE
           PREMISES OF SOMEONE WHO IS *NOT* A
           SUSPECT? 69

Chapter 8
Drafting a Search Warrant: Information Sources 71
    8.1   MAY POLICE USE INFORMATION SUPPLIED BY
           PRIVATE CITIZENS? 71
    8.2   MAY POLICE USE INFORMATION SUPPLIED TO
           THEM BY *INFORMANTS?* 72
    8.3   MAY POLICE USE *HEARSAY* INFORMATION TO
           OBTAIN A WARRANT? 73
    8.4   MAY POLICE USE INFORMATION SUPPLIED BY
           ANONYMOUS TIPSTERS? 74
    8.5   WHAT IS THE BEST WAY TO USE INFORMATION
           PROVIDED BY A *JOHN DOE* INFORMANT? 75

8.6   Do Police Need to Use an *Informant's Actual Name* When Applying for a Search Warrant? 75

Chapter 9
Drafting a Search Warrant: Requirements 77

9.1   What Information *Must be Included* in a Warrant? 78
9.2   What Information Ought to be *Left Out* of a Warrant? 79
9.3   How *Specific* Must a Warrant be in Describing the *Things to be Seized?* 80
9.4   How *Specific* Must a Warrant be in *Describing the Place to be Searched?* . . . 81

Chapter 10
Post Arrest Investigation 83

10.1   When Must Police Give a Suspect his Miranda Warnings? 83
10.2   Under What Circumstances May a Suspect Waive His Miranda Rights? 84
10.3   Does a Suspect's Miranda Waiver Have to be in Writing to be Valid? 85
10.4   Are Police *Required* to Provide a Suspect an Attorney if he asks, "Do You Think I Need a Lawyer?" 85
10.5   May Police Question a Suspect about a Crime If He Is *in Custody for Another Crime?* 86
10.6   Do Police Have to Provide a Suspect an Attorney for a Line-up? 87
10.7   Is it Permissible for Police to *Lie* to a Suspect to Gain His Confession? 88

Table of Authorities 89

Index 95

Dedication

*This book is dedicated
in loving memory of
my brother Rafael Medina
(1964-2006)*

i

Acknowledgments

I would like to acknowledge and express my sincere appreciation to the following people who have helped me, each in their own way, to complete this book:

My wife Leslie Medina, whose patience and support has been invaluable. To my dad Roberto Medina who taught me to look with a critical eye and never accept any idea without first "looking under the hood." To the following people who shared with me their knowledge and inspiration: Ellen Mandeltort (Assistant Illinois Attorney General: Supervising Attorney for the Criminal Division) along with Mark Shlifka (Cook County Felony Trial Division: Wing Supervisor) two of the best trial attorneys I have ever seen. The Honorable Judge Karen Thompson Tobin who has the perfect combination of legal knowledge, judicial temperament and uncanny sense of justice. Deputy Chief of the Streamwood Police James Keegan who helped me cut my teeth on my first stint on Felony Review. Attorney's Scott Grogan and Heather Beard. My partners at the Cook County States Attorney's Office: (ASA) Lynn Palac, (ASA) Shari Chandra and (ASA) Shandra Leary, their intelligence is matched only by their great sense of humor. Also (ASA) Judy Weldon, (ASA) Ruth Howes, (ASA) James Pontrellie, (ASA) Rich Karwaczka, (ASA: Retired) John Lombardi, (ASA) Mike Gerber, Thomas Byrne (3rd District Supervisor), Steven Rosenblum (3rd District Deputy Supervisor), (ASA) Marilyn Hite-Ross, and the wonderful support staff at the Cook County State's Attorneys Office, Denise Armstrong, Mary Stream, Debbie Poremba and Mary Stacy.

Matthew Joseph Medina received his Juris Doctor degree from the University of Illinois College of Law and has been a member of the Illinois Bar since 1996. He is an Assistant Cook County State's Attorney. He recently completed a tour of duty in the Felony Review Unit where he analyzed, screened and charged felony cases coming out of 27 police jurisdictions, approved and edited search warrants and interviewed suspects and witnesses for violent crimes and Class X felonies. The Felony Review Unit also provides legal counsel to police command staff on constitutional law issues respecting their investigations. In his free time, he teaches Criminal Law and Procedure at Northwestern Business College and spends time with his wife, Leslie, and step-son, Zack in Winfield, Illinois.

The following is a practical guide for law enforcement personnel and local prosecutors. This guide answers specific search and seizure questions that arise in the everyday practice of law enforcement. This guide is designed to provide succinct answers to these questions in a manner that is user friendly and non-academic. The case citations in this book are up-to-date as to the date of this book's publication. Most of the answers in this book come from United States Supreme Court cases or the highest Federal Court authority on the particular question. This means that the answers are authoritative in most jurisdictions for most purposes. Local rules and state constitutions may, in some instances, provide more protection to the suspect than is provided by the federal constitution. So check your local rules.

The most important function of police, from a prosecutor's perspective, is to gather useful evidence for the eventual prosecution and conviction of criminals. Evidence is most useful to the prosecution when it is admissible at trial. Lawyers, judges, attorney's and law professors argue about the fine points of Constitutional law and interpretation; it is the cop on the street, however, that actually practices Constitutional law. This is why police, more than anyone, need to have a firm grasp on search and seizure rules.

The Fourth Amendment to the United States Constitution provides that: "The right of the people to be secure in their persons, houses, papers, and effects, against unreasonable searches and seizures, shall not be violated, and no Warrants shall issue, but upon probable cause, supported by Oath or affirmation, and particularly describing the place to be searched and the persons or things to be seized." If police violate this Amendment, the state may be prohibited from using this evidence at a defendant's trial. Because the Fourth Amendment explicitly applies to the federal government, the Supreme Court later said that this Amendment now applies to the states through the Due Process Clause of the Fourteenth Amendment to the

United States Constitution. What does this mean? The Fourth Amendment applies to both federal and state authorities.

What are the three primary forms of evidence police gather?

First - Police gather physical evidence: DNA, fingerprints, drugs, documents, blood, crime-scene debris and countless other articles of interest to the prosecution.

Second - Police gather suspects. That is, they arrest people.

Third - Police gather statements: witness statements, statements from informants, statements from bystanders, and statements from defendants.

Police gather the first and second type of evidence using their main tool of the trade—searches and seizures. Police search and seize evidence sometimes with the authority of a court-authorized warrant in hand; and sometimes police search and seize evidence without the benefit of a court-authorized warrant. The Fourth Amendment governs this decision. Therefore, the main question police need to answer when they are searching, seizing or arresting a suspect is: "under what circumstances am I legally required to obtain a warrant?"

The third type of evidence police gather, statements from defendants, is governed by a different set of Constitutional rules. Police must learn the rules associated with the Fifth, Sixth and the Fourteenth Amendments. Of these rules, it is the Fifth Amendment that is most applicable to day-to-day police work. The relevant part of the Fifth Amendment to the United States Constitution provides that "No person shall ... be compelled in any criminal case to be a witness against himself..." The language of this Amendment seems clear enough, but what does it actually mean in real life situations? When must police read a suspect his Miranda warnings? Under what circumstances may a suspect waive his Miranda rights? This book will answer these and other questions relating to the arrest, search, seizure and questioning of suspects.

Part I

WARRANTLESS
SEARCHES AND SEIZURES

THE FOURTH AMENDMENT IS NOT, of course, a guarantee against *ALL* searches and seizures, but only against *UNREASONABLE* searches and seizures. *United States v. Sharpe*, 470 U.S. 675, 681 (1985) (Emphasis added)

1.1 WHEN DOES THE FOURTH AMENDMENT APPLY AND WHY DOES IT MATTER?

ANSWER

The Fourth Amendment applies *only* when the *police* (or other governmental actors) conduct a "search" or a "seizure" or when someone acting *on behalf of* the Police conduct a "search" or a "seizure." A search occurs when the police interfere with a suspect's reasonable expectation of privacy. [1] A seizure of property occurs when police engage in a *meaningful interference* with a suspect's possessory interest in his property. [2] If neither occurs then the Fourth Amendment does not apply. Why is it important for a police officer to know if the Fourth Amendment applies to a situation? The answer is simple. If the Fourth Amendment applies to a particular course of conduct by the police then they must follow a set of rules. What are those rules? If the Fourth Amendment applies, police need a warrant based on probable cause, or some exception to the warrant requirement. If the police do not follow these rules, the evidence that they gather may be *excluded from consideration at trial* under what is known as the *exclusionary rule.* [3] The *exclusionary rule* applies to searches and seizures conducted by both federal and state law enforcement personnel.

3

ANALYSIS

The first question a police officer or prosecutor must ask is, "Does the Fourth Amendment even apply in this situation?" What this question means is "Does this course of conduct meet the *legal definition* of a search or seizure?" If that action does not meet the legal definition of search or seizure then the Fourth Amendment rules do not apply. If this is the case, there is no need to worry that the evidence gathered will be suppressed (at least for violation of the Fourth Amendment). The Fourth Amendment rules apply only to the police and other state actors. *The Fourth Amendment does not apply to private people* such as security guards or ordinary citizens unless they are acting at the direction of the police or other state actors.

 POLICE TIP

When deciding whether the Fourth Amendment applies to a particular situation, ask yourself the following questions:

- *Does this activity constitute a search?*

- *Does this activity constitute a seizure?*

- *Is the person searching or seizing a police officer or other governmental actor?*

- *If the person searching or seizing is not a police officer or other governmental actor, ask: "Is that person acting on behalf of the police or governmental actor?"*

If you answer **YES** to any of these questions you must follow the Fourth Amendment rules.

1.2 WHEN DOES THE FOURTH AMENDMENT *NOT* APPLY?

ANSWER

The Fourth Amendment does not apply to the following: Searches conducted by *private individuals* without police or government involvement; police examination of things that are exposed to the *public view*; searches or seizures of property that has been *abandoned*; search and seizures based on *voluntary consent* (under most circumstances), police *dog sniffs*. [4] (Other such activities that only detect the presence or absence of contraband and police duplication of searches conducted by private individuals.)

ANALYSIS

The bottom line is this: The courts have determined that the Fourth Amendment is only a limitation on *governmental* activities and that the Fourth Amendment only prohibits *unreasonable* searches or seizures. If a person does not have a *reasonable expectation of privacy* in the subject matter of the police search or seizure, the Fourth Amendment does not apply.

 POLICE TIP

The "plain view" doctrine will support a warrantless seizure of property if:

- Police are *lawfully in the place* where the property was plainly seen
- The property is in *plain view*
- The property's *incriminating nature* is immediately apparent
- Police have *lawful right of access* to the object itself

1.3	WHAT CONSTITUTES ABANDONED PROPERTY?

ANSWER

The test for abandonment is whether an individual has retained any reasonable expectation of privacy in the item. [5]

ANALYSIS

Why is it important for police to determine whether property they search or seize is abandoned property? If property is abandoned, police may search or seize that property without warrant and without any justification. In determining whether property has been abandoned, courts look at the totality of the circumstances and consider the following factors: (1) whether the suspect denied ownership of the property; and (2) whether he or she physically relinquished ownership in the property. Whether abandonment has occurred is determined on the basis of objective facts known to the officer at the time, not on the basis of the suspect's subjective intent. [6] In the following examples courts have found that the property in question was abandoned and was therefore subject to warrantless seizure:

- Even though the defendant claimed ownership of a portfolio in a backpack, while falsely denying ownership of the backpack, the backpack itself was abandoned, therefore the motion to suppress the evidence was properly denied. [7]

- A teacher did not have a reasonable expectation of privacy in his former desk or file cabinets because they were located in a public school classroom open to students and colleagues. [8]

- Defendant had no reasonable expectation of privacy in undeveloped film that spilled out of defendant's car after an accident. [9]

- Police creation of a ruse, such as a drug checkpoint, to cause a defendant to abandon item was not illegal, therefore the finding that the property was abandoned was proper. [10]

- Where defendant expressly and implicitly denied ownership of any luggage in an overhead rack on a bus, abandonment justified agents in searching an unclaimed suitcase from the overhead rack despite a tag with defendant's name. [11]

- Defendant never submitted to officers' authority; thus, the gun that the suspect discarded during the middle of a police chase was voluntarily abandoned and subject to a warrantless seizure. [12]

POLICE TIP

If the property is abandoned there is no need for a warrant or even probable cause to seize that property.

POLICE TIP

Police are only permitted to seize four types of property. First, police may seize contraband, that is, property that people do not have a right to possess in the first place. Second, police may seize fruits of a crime. Third, police may seize items used to commit a crime. Fourth, police may seize mere evidence, that is, evidence that relates in some way to the crime or evidence that may be useful in proving some aspect of the crime.

1.4   WHAT IS A SEARCH?

ANSWER

A search occurs when police intrude on a person's *reasonable expectation of privacy.* [13] A person must have an actual subjective expectation of privacy and that expectation must be one that society considers *reasonable.*

ANALYSIS

A search is not what you think it is. Well, it is, but it is more. When most people think of the term *search* in the context of police activity, they picture the police actually *physically* rummaging through someone's house or possessions. Is this a search? Yes—it can be. However, the term search has a specific legal definition that can be much more expansive than just the physical rummaging through a person's property. A search occurs when the police intrude on a person's *reasonable expectation of privacy*. What does that definition mean to an officer on the street? It means that there does not necessarily need to be a physical intrusion into a person's property for a search to occur. On the other hand, even if there is a physical intrusion on a person's property, there may not be a search. The United States Supreme Court in the case *United States v. Katz* said: "What this means to the officer on the streets is that oftentimes what seems to be a search is not a search at all...What a person knowingly exposes to the public, even in his home or office, is not a subject of Fourth Amendment protection... but what he seeks to preserve as private, even in an area accessible to the public, may be constitutionally protected." [14] The following are examples where courts found that a "search" did not occur:

- If an inspection by police does not intrude upon a legitimate expectation of privacy, there is no "search." [15]

- The exposure of luggage, which is located in a public place, to a trained canine does not constitute a "search." [16]

- Ultraviolet light examination does not constitute a Fourth Amendment search. [17]

- Eavesdropping by an agent from a motel walkway, within earshot of the defendant's open motel room, did not constitute a search because "it is not a 'search' to observe, that which occurs *openly* in public." [18]

- The inspection of tires on a motor vehicle, performed by police officers entitled to be on the property where the vehicle was located, which in no way damaged the tires or the vehicle and was limited to determining the serial numbers of the tires was not a search within the Fourth Amendment. [19]

- Fourth Amendment does not require the police traveling in the public airways at an altitude of 400 feet to obtain a warrant in order to observe what is visible to the naked eye. [20]

- A dog sniff is not a search and no probable cause or reasonable suspicion is necessary to conduct it, because it is minimally intrusive and neither requires entry nor subjects any items except contraband to police scrutiny. [21]

 POLICE TIP

If a search (as defined by law) has not occurred, police do not need a warrant based on probable cause or any exception to the warrant requirement. The Fourth Amendment and the exclusionary rule simply do not apply.

POLICE TIP

Even when officers have no basis for suspecting a particular individual, they may generally ask questions of that individual, examine the individual's identification, and request consent to search.

1.5   WHAT CONSTITUTES A SEIZURE OF PROPERTY?

ANSWER

A seizure of property occurs when the police commit a *meaningful interference* with a person's possessory interest in their property. [22]

ANALYSIS

Police must possess a warrant (or some exception to the warrant requirement) to justify a seizure of a person's property. This is why it is important for police to know what exactly is a seizure. Because if their activities to not constitute a *seizure*, then *no justification* is needed to seize the property. If there is a *meaningful interference* with a person's interest in their property then there is a seizure. The main question a police officer must ask is, "Was there a *meaningful interference* with a person's possessory interest in their property?" If the answer to the above question is no, a *seizure* has not occurred, therefore the Fourth Amendment rules do not apply.

POLICE TIP

Police activities that constitute a meaningful interference in a suspect's possessory interest in their property:

- Officer takes suspect's jacket off a park bench and rips the inside pockets out in search for drugs
- Officer confiscates suspect's wallet and takes it to the police station for a temporary inspection
- Officer tows suspect's car after a driving under the influence charge

Police activities that do not constitute a meaningful interference with a suspect's possessory interest in their property:

- Officer picks up suspect's wallet, looks at it and puts it back down
- Officer visually inspects suspect's property from a public street through an open window
- Officer picks up a note written by suspect, reads it, and puts it back down (this may be a search however?)

Chapter 2

Preliminary Investigation: Stopping & Questioning People

In dealing with the *rapidly unfolding* and often *dangerous* situations on city streets the police are in need of an escalating set of *flexible responses*, graduated in relation to the amount of information they possess. *Terry v. Ohio*, 392 U.S. 1, 10 (1968) (Emphasis added)

Introduction

Simply talking with people on the street can provide a rich source of intelligence on crime in a neighborhood. Police have many functions that range from community caretaking to the apprehension of dangerous criminals. All of these functions require a great deal of contact with citizens. Police-citizen contact can range from the casual to the coercive. Many police investigations involving serious crime begin with casual type of police-citizen contact. Often during these non-coercive interactions, an officer may develop reasons to investigate further. These reasons sometimes develop into suspicions—and later to probable cause. The following chapter will answer some basic questions that arise during the very preliminary stages of an investigation. What rules must police adhere to when they seek to stop, question, or arrest an individual?

2.1 WHAT ARE THE THREE TYPES OF POLICE-CITIZEN CONTACT?

ANSWER

The courts recognize three types of police-citizen contact:

First, a consensual encounter between police and a person on the street;

Second, a limited investigatory stop or seizure based upon reasonable suspicion;

Third, an arrest based on probable cause.

ANALYSIS

It is important for police to be able to distinguish between the three types of police-citizen contact. The reason that this distinction is important is that each progressive level of police intrusion upon a citizen's privacy or security requires police to have greater levels of *objective justification*. The first level of police-citizen contact is an *encounter*. This contact requires no justification at all. Police can attempt to talk with whomever they want on the street without any justification. Of course, the person on the street has a right not to cooperate. The second level is the stop "*Terry* stop" or the brief seizure. Here police need some (very limited) objective justification. The courts require police to have "reasonable suspicion" that criminal activity is afoot to justify a brief seizure of an individual. The third level of police citizen contact, the arrest, requires police to justify their action with "probable cause" to believe that a crime was committed and the suspect committed that crime.

POLICE TIP

You are *not required* to tell a person that they are "free to leave" in order for the interaction to be an *encounter* (requiring no justification). However, if you do tell a person that they are "free to leave," that statement will be persuasive evidence showing that the interaction was indeed *consensual.*

2.2 WHAT CONSTITUTES A CONSENSUAL POLICE ENCOUNTER?

ANSWER

An encounter takes place when there is a *consensual* interaction between a person and the police in a public place. Because an encounter is not a seizure, police need *no justification* for an encounter.

ANALYSIS

The first question an officer should ask is: "Is this interaction an *encounter* or is it a *seizure?*" Not every personal interaction between policemen and citizens involves a *seizure* of persons. [23] If the police-citizen interaction is consensual in nature, that is, a *reasonable person* innocent of any crime would feel free to leave; the Fourth Amendment does not apply. The courts have interpreted the *reasonable person* standard in a manner quite favorable to the police. Police have great latitude to question individuals without implicating the Fourth Amendment. In the following examples courts found that the police-citizen contact was an *encounter* requiring police to have no objective justification:

- Police did not *seize* suspects when they boarded the bus and began questioning passengers. The officers gave the passengers no reason to believe that they were *required* to answer questions. The officers did not show any weapons or make any intimidating movements, they left the aisle free so that passengers could exit, and spoke to them one by one in a polite, quiet voice. Nothing the officer said would have suggested to a reasonable person that he was barred from leaving or terminating the encounter. [24]

- Law enforcement officers do not violate the Fourth Amendment by merely approaching individuals on the street or other public place and asking him if he is willing to answer some questions...if the person is willing to listen. [25]

- A seizure does not occur when officers approach an individual and, after identifying themselves, request an interview and an opportunity to inspect the individual's driver's license and airline ticket. [26]

- Even when law enforcement officers have no basis for suspecting a particular individual, they may pose questions, ask for identification, and request consent to search luggage—provided they do not induce cooperation by coercive means. [27]

- Police do not have to inform the person questioned that he is free to leave in order for the interaction to qualify as consensual. [28]

- It is unreasonable to have an expectation of privacy in an object required by law to be located in a place ordinarily in plain view from the exterior of the automobile. [VIN number, License Plate etc...] [29]

- It is not a seizure for an officer to walk up to and talk to a person in a public place, including a person in a parked car. A policeman's approach to a parked vehicle is not a seizure if the officer inquires of the occupant in a conversational manner, does not order the person to do something, and does not demand a response. [30]

- When evaluating the totality of the circumstances, we have noted that a police-citizen encounter does not become a seizure simply because citizens may feel an inherent social pressure to cooperate with the police. [31]

2.3	WHAT IS A *TERRY* STOP?

ANSWER

A *Terry* stop is a brief investigatory seizure of a person. A *Terry* stop occurs when the officer, by means of *physical force or show of authority*, has in some way restrained the liberty of a citizen. [32] A person has been "seized" within the meaning of the Fourth Amendment only if, in view of all of the circumstances surrounding the incident, a reasonable person would have believed that he was not free to leave. [33] The Fourth Amendment applies to *brief investigatory stops* of persons or vehicles that fall short of traditional arrest. [34] In order for police to temporarily seize a person they need to have *reasonable suspicion* that criminal activity is afoot. [35] An investigatory stop must be justified by some *objective* manifestation that the person stopped is, or is about to be, engaged in criminal activity. [36] A *Terry* stop is brief and to the point. Because of this, it requires less justification than a full scale arrest requires. If during the stop an officer develops more than reasonable suspicion (probable cause) he may then conduct a more extensive search or seizure based on this new information.

ANALYSIS

Courts look at two things when they determine whether an investigative stop was reasonable:

First, they examine whether the officer's action was justified at its *inception.*

Second, the courts will look at whether the officer's action was reasonably related in *scope* to the circumstances that justified the interference in the first place. [37]

The courts will consider the interaction a *seizure* and not an *encounter* if the police become coercive in their actions towards a citizen. [38] Any touching of a suspect constitutes a seizure. [39] However, if the seizure occurs by *a show of authority* there must be a *submission* to the assertion of authority for it to constitute a seizure. [40]

 POLICE TIP

Consider these factors when deciding whether police interaction with a citizen is an encounter (requiring no justification) or a seizure (requiring reasonable suspicion). The following actions will make a seizure more likely:

- Blocking suspect's movement
- Showing force through the presence of many officers or the drawing of a weapon
- Taking a suspect's identification and keeping it for an extended period of time
- Use of threatening language towards the suspect
- Extended questioning for a long period of time

POLICE TIP

During a *Terry* stop police may do any of the following:

- Request suspect supply identification
- Briefly question suspect on scene
- Radio station to verify suspect's information
- Request consent to conduct a comprehensive search
- Transport suspect a short distance for a show-up

2.4   WHAT IS *REASONABLE SUSPICION?*

ANSWER

Courts look at the *totality of the circumstances* of each case to see whether the detaining officer has a *particularized* and *objective basis* for suspecting wrongdoing. [41] If there are facts supporting a reasonable suspicion that a person has committed (or is about to commit) a criminal offense, that person may be stopped in order to identify him, to question him briefly, or to detain him briefly while attempting to obtain additional information. [42]

ANALYSIS

It is difficult to say precisely what is "reasonable suspicion." It is a commonsense and non-technical consideration. [43] One thing that can be said for sure is that *reasonable suspicion* is not a high standard. It is *less* than probable cause. [44] The Fourth Amendment does not require a policeman who lacks the precise level of information necessary for probable cause to arrest to simply shrug his shoulders and allow a crime to occur or a criminal to escape. [45] Police may act to *briefly* detain an individual based on *less* than probable cause in order for them to obtain probable cause to arrest. If the officer does not learn facts rising to the level of probable cause, the individual stopped must be permitted to go on his way. [46] The following are some examples of factors and situations that courts will consider when determining whether there was *reasonable suspicion*:

NOTE: The principal components of a determination of reasonable suspicion will be the events that occurred leading up to the stop or search—not after the fact discoveries. [47]

☐ Suspect's presence in "high crime" area [48]

☐ Sudden unprovoked flight upon seeing police [49]

☐ Nervous and evasive behavior [50]

☐ Conflicting or implausible stories [51]

☐ Even *lawful* behavior susceptible to an *innocent explanation* that is viewed by an officer, based on his or her experience to be suspicious, can be a factor that gives rise to reasonable suspicion [52]

☐ A police officer may draw inferences based on his *own experience* in deciding whether probable cause or reasonable suspicion exists [53]

☐ Deliberately furtive actions and flight at the approach of strangers or law officers are strong indicia [of intent], and when coupled with specific knowledge on the part of the officer relating the suspect to evidence of crime, they are proper factors to be considered [by police] [54]

POLICE TIP

Even though the reasonable suspicion standard is low, police must still rely on particular facts to justify a stop. The justification cannot be based on "a hunch."

2.5	WHAT JUSTIFICATION IS NEEDED TO CONDUCT A BRIEF PAT DOWN SEARCH OF A SUSPECT FOR WEAPONS?

ANSWER

Where police observe unusual conduct which lead them, based on their experience, that criminal activity may be afoot, *and* that the persons that they are dealing with may be armed and dangerous, police are entitled to conduct a *carefully limited search* of the outer clothing of such persons in an *attempt to discover weapons.* [55]

ANALYSIS

Officers must keep in mind that the pat down search is conducted for the *sole purpose* of officer safety. This is *not* a search for evidence. If police accidentally find evidence of a crime as a result of the pat down search, that evidence can be used against the suspect at trial. However, police are *not permitted* to manipulate the suspect's pockets or clothing in order to search for evidence of crime. [56]

 POLICE TIP

Police need 2 *independent* justifications in order to conduct a lawful *"Terry* stop *and* frisk."
- First, police must have reasonable suspicion to *stop* the suspect.
- Second, police must have reason to believe that the suspect is *armed and dangerous* to justify the *frisk* for weapons.

The following are examples of factors that (along with others) may give rise to reasonable suspicion that a suspect is armed and dangerous:

☐ Suspect is involved in selling drugs ("where there are drugs there are almost always guns") [57]

☐ Suspect was acting nervously *and* refused to take his hands out of his pockets after officer requested that he do so [58]

☐ Observable bulge under suspect's clothing [59]

☐ Aggressive behavior by defendant towards officer [60]

☐ Larger number of suspects in relation to police [61]

☐ Relative isolation of officer and presence of multiple possible offenders [62]

The following factors give rise to an automatic right to search a suspect:

• Police have an automatic right to order a person out of a vehicle for police safety after a proper traffic stop. [63] This automatic right also extends to passengers of a lawfully stopped vehicle [64]

- Where police reasonably suspect a person is armed and dangerous they may conduct a protective search of the passenger compartment of a car during the course of a *Terry* stop [65]

 POLICE TIP

A frisk of a suspect for weapons may turn up evidence of a crime (like drugs) only if that evidence was *immediately apparent without manipulating the item. Minnesota v. Dickerson*, 508 U.S. 366, 378-379 (1993)

2.6	WHEN DOES A *TERRY* STOP BECOME AN *ARREST* AND WHY DOES IT MATTER?

ANSWER

The question a police officer must ask is whether the suspect's detention exceeded: "a *brief* stop, interrogation and, under proper circumstances, a brief check for weapons." [66] Whether a particular detention is deemed a *Terry* stop or an *arrest* is of great importance because that decision will often determine whether the police conduct was lawful or not. If it is concluded that the detention was only a "stop" it will be lawful even though there was no probable cause. If, under the same circumstances, it is determined that the detention is an arrest, it will not be lawful unless there is probable cause. [67]

ANALYSIS

23

If police exceed the scope permissible under a brief investigatory stop (*Terry* stop), the courts will deem the detention an arrest. Courts look at the scope of the investigation and the length of the suspect's detention to determine whether a stop has become an arrest. Like most Fourth Amendment inquiries, courts look at the totality of the circumstances when they decide whether a particular stop has become an arrest. The broader the scope of the police investigation and the lengthier the detention, the more likely the courts will find that the detention is an arrest, therefore requiring police to have *probable cause.*

The following situations require police to have *probable cause*:

- Moving a suspect to a custodial area for further questioning [68]

- Bringing a suspect to the station without his consent [69]

- Detaining a suspect in a police car without his consent [70]

The following examples require police to have only reasonable suspicion:

- Under ordinary circumstances, drawing weapons and using handcuffs are not part of a *Terry* stop, however, courts have permitted the use of intrusive means (like drawing of a gun) to effect a *Terry* stop where the police have information that the suspect is currently armed or the stop closely follows a violent crime [71]

- A border suspect's handcuffed 30- to 40-yard walk to a border security office did not turn his detention into an arrest, where the suspect was told the handcuffs were only temporary [72]

- Blocking suspect's vehicle with two police cruisers, approaching with guns drawn, ordering suspects to put their hands on dashboard and subsequently frisking them did not constitute arrest [73]

Fourth Amendment jurisprudence has consistently accorded law enforcement officials *greater latitude* in exercising their duties in *public places.* For example, although a warrant presumptively is required for a felony arrest in a suspect's home, the *Fourth Amendment permits warrantless arrests* in *public places* where an officer has *probable cause* to believe that a *felony* has occurred. *United States v. Watson,* 423 U.S. 411, 416 (Emphasis added)

Introduction

The law gives police unquestioned authority to arrest suspects under the proper circumstances. This arrest power—a power that is also given to *ordinary citizens* under the proper circumstances—is an awesome responsibility. Being placed under arrest, even temporarily, is the ultimate deprivation of liberty. Because of this, police must follow rules that balance a citizen's right to maintain his liberty, against the State's right to protect its citizens from dangerous criminals.

We will learn in this chapter the rules that police must follow to make a lawful arrest of a suspect. We will learn how *public arrests* differ from arrests that take place in a suspect's *home.* This chapter will answer some basic questions about warrantless arrests of individuals, the police arrest-power rule, and the standard of probable cause relating to the stop, investigation and arrest of suspects.

> **3.1   WHAT CONSTITUTES AN *ARREST* AND WHAT *JUSTIFICATION* DO POLICE NEED TO MAKE A *WARRANTLESS PUBLIC ARREST*?**

ANSWER

An officer arrests a suspect by *either* the application of physical force—however slight—*or*, where that is absent, submission to an officer's "show of authority" to restrain the subject's liberty. [74] A warrantless arrest of an individual in a public place for a felony, or a misdemeanor committed in the officer's presence, is consistent with the Fourth Amendment if the arrest is supported by *probable cause*. [75]

ANALYSIS

It is important for an officer to know where the *investigatory stop* ends and the *arrest* begins. The reason is that for an *arrest* an officer needs to have *probable cause* to believe that a crime was (or is being) committed and *this suspect* committed the crime. The lesser standard of *reasonable suspicion* applies to the less intrusive *temporary seizures* of suspects (*Terry* stops).

 POLICE TIP

Fourth Amendment *prohibits* police from making a *warrantless* and *nonconsensual* entry into a suspect's *home* in order to make a routine felony arrest. *Payton v. New York*, 445 U.S. 573, 576 (1980)

POLICE TIP

Police do not need a warrant to apprehend a suspected *felon* in a *public place*. All that is required is that you have *probable cause* to believe that a crime was committed and this suspect committed that crime. *United States v. Watson*, 423 U.S. 411, 417 (1976)

3.2	WHEN IS IT PERMISSIBLE FOR POLICE TO ARREST A SUSPECT WITHOUT A WARRANT?

ANSWER

A law enforcement officer may arrest a person *without a warrant* if the officer has [probable] cause to believe that such person has committed a *felony*, a *misdemeanor committed in the officer's presence* or a *misdemeanor that necessitates immediate arrest* of a suspect because of possible injury to himself or the public. [76]

ANALYSIS

Like any other seizure, courts *prefer* police have a warrant when they arrest a suspect. And if the arrest takes place in a home, an arrest warrant (or search warrant) is required.

POLICE TIP

If supported by probable cause, police may arrest an individual *without a warrant* in a public place for a felony, or a misdemeanor committed in the officer's presence. *United States v. Watson*, 423 U.S. 411, 424, (1976)

3.3   WHAT IS *PROBABLE CAUSE* IN THE CONTEXT OF AN ARREST?

ANSWER

Probable cause exists where the facts and circumstances within the officer's knowledge are sufficient in themselves to warrant a man of reasonable caution to believe that an offense has been or is being committed." [77] These facts and circumstances must arise from the officer's personal knowledge *or* they must be derived from reasonably *trustworthy information.* [78] *Probable cause* only differs from *reasonable suspicion* in degree. This means that in both circumstances police must have *objective facts* to support their suspicions. The *probable cause* standard is simply a more *complete picture* of their suspicions.

ANALYSIS

There is no precise definition of probable cause because it deals with *probabilities* and depends on the *totality of the circumstances.* What we do know is that there has to be a *reasonable objective basis* to believe in the guilt of the person arrested. [79] This does *not* mean, however, that at the time of the arrest police need enough evidence to sustain a conviction at trial. In fact, it doesn't. The standard of probable cause is a *much lower* standard than proof beyond a reasonable doubt.

POLICE TIP

Remember and record in your report *all* of the suspicious behavior engaged in by the suspect *before* the stop or arrest. This should include even seemingly innocent behavior, which, based on your experience, could be interpreted as unusual or incriminating. Court's look at the *totality of the circumstances* when they determine whether a stop or arrest was legally justified.

3.4 WHEN DO POLICE NEED *PROBABLE CAUSE* TO CONTINUE THEIR DETENTION OF A SUSPECT?

ANSWER

Police need *probable cause* to place a suspect under *arrest*.

ANALYSIS

A greater level of justification is needed for an officer to *arrest* a suspect than is needed for him to *temporarily stop* a suspect for investigatory purposes.

The following factors will likely turn an investigatory stop into an arrest requiring *probable cause*:

— Forced movement to a custodial area

— Movement to a police vehicle

— Taking suspect to the police station

— Forced movement for identification

— Time limitation between stop and arrest

— Communication to the suspect that he is under arrest

3.5   WHAT INFORMATION CAN POLICE USE AS A BASIS FOR *PROBABLE CAUSE* TO ARREST A SUSPECT?

ANSWER

Police may use *personal observations*, information derived from *reliable* or *trustworthy* informants, information given to them by other police, police dispatch, citizens, or information provided by the suspect himself to use as a basis for *probable cause.*

ANALYSIS

Police can use all sorts of information to serve as a basis for probable cause to arrest a suspect. If the information that police use is from their own personal observation, other police or regular citizens (non-informants), the courts will be more inclined to treat the information as a reliable basis for *probable cause.*

The following are examples of observations an officer may use, *in combination with other evidence*, to develop probable cause (officers may legally stop and question an individual based on these factors):

— Courts look at the *totality of circumstances* not factors in isolation [80]

— Even if there are *innocent explanations* for suspect's actions, those actions may serve as a basis [81]

— Courts tolerate *reasonable mistakes* by police in their probable cause determination [82]

- Courts consider *training and experience* of officer [83]

- Police may consider what *other officers tell them* [84]

- Police may make use of *hearsay informants* (see 3.6)

- Police may consider *flight or furtive conduct* [85]

- Police may consider suspect's *evasive answers*, refusal to answer or recantation of story [86]

- Nature of the area where suspect is observed (*high drug crime area*) is a relevant factor [87]

3.6   MAY *PROBABLE CAUSE* BE DERIVED FROM AN *ANONYMOUS TIP?*

ANSWER

Yes.

ANALYSIS

Anonymous tips can be used as a basis to begin an independent police investigation that results in probable cause. The key to using an anonymous tip is for the police to *independently corroborate* as much of the tip as possible before they stop, search or arrest the suspect. Courts consider the *totality of circumstances* when they decide whether an anonymous tip was sufficiently corroborated. [88]

- Based on an anonymous telephone tip, police stopped respondent's vehicle. A consensual search of the car revealed drugs. The issue is whether the tip, *as corroborated by independent police work*, exhibited sufficient indicia of reliability to provide *reasonable suspicion* to make the investigatory stop. The United State's Supreme Court held that it did. [89]

- (Anonymous letter) Courts look at *the totality of circumstances* when deciding whether an anonymous letter was sufficiently corroborated. [90]

- Courts value of *corroboration of details* of an informant's tip by *independent police work.* [91]

- An anonymous tip that a person is carrying a gun is, without more information, insufficient to justify a police officer's stop and frisk of that person. [92]

3.7   WHAT IS A *SEARCH INCIDENT TO ARREST?*

ANSWER

Police may search a suspect without a warrant incident to a lawful arrest of that suspect. This means that a suspect may be searched at the time, or shortly after he is placed under arrest. This rule is automatic. Police need no additional justification to search a suspect once that suspect is placed under arrest. Officers may search *the person* of the arrestee by virtue of the lawful arrest and may also search the *area within the control* of the arrestee. [93]

ANALYSIS

The search incident to arrest rule has been broadened by the courts over the years to include an area well beyond the grab-area of the suspect. When police have made a lawful custodial arrest of an occupant in an automobile (or recent occupant) they may search the passenger compartment of that automobile incident to arrest. [94] Search incident to arrest must be conducted *within a short time* of the arrest to fall within this exception to the warrant requirement. [95] Some courts will extend the time frame if police are continuing the process of their investigation over an extended time frame. [96] To be safe, police should conduct their search incident to arrest contemporaneously with the arrest.

 POLICE TIP

Search incident to arrest of an occupant of an automobile:

- Police may search passenger compartment of automobile
- Police may search the suspect
- Police may search suspect's immediate surroundings

If a car is readily mobile and probable cause exists to believe it contains contraband, the Fourth Amendment thus permits police to search the vehicle without more information. *Pennsylvania v. Labron*, 518 U.S. 938, 940 (1996)

Introduction

Police do not need a warrant to stop or search a vehicle. The United States Supreme Court has decided that people have a lesser expectation of privacy in their vehicles. If a person has a lesser expectation of privacy, she has, therefore, lesser protections under the Fourth Amendment of the Constitution. Because of this lesser expectation of privacy, police only need reasonable suspicion to stop a vehicle and probable cause to search a vehicle. The following chapter will provide answers to some basic questions associated with vehicle searches.

4.1	WHAT JUSTIFICATION DO POLICE NEED TO STOP A VEHICLE?

ANSWER

All stops of vehicles are considered seizures. Police may stop a vehicle based on *reasonable suspicion*.

ANALYSIS

Police may stop an individual for minor traffic offenses including non-moving violations like equipment violations. Police must remember, however, that once the original basis for the stop is concluded police must allow the suspect to leave unless during the stop additional suspicion is gained. Police may use the same factors set forth in [Sec. 3.5] as a basis to stop an individual in an automobile.

4.2	**WHEN IS IT PERMISSIBLE FOR POLICE TO SEARCH A VEHICLE WITHOUT A WARRANT?**

ANSWER

There are a few different justifications police can use to search vehicles. The Fourth Amendment permits police to search a vehicle without a warrant as long as they have *probable cause* to believe that the vehicle contains evidence. [97] In this case, police may search anywhere in the vehicle that may contain the object of their search. If police are searching for drugs they may search anywhere drugs may be hidden. Police may also search the *passenger compartment* of a vehicle after they have made a lawful custodial arrest of its occupant (or recent occupant). [98] The search incident to arrest justification extends the search only to the passenger compartment of the vehicle and therefore does not include the right to search the trunk without independent probable cause. Search incident to arrest is a more *limited search* than a search based on probable cause. But a search incident to arrest is automatic. After police arrest a suspect they do not need additional justification to search the passenger compartment of his vehicle incident to arrest.

ANALYSIS

- Where defendant exited a vehicle prior to being contacted by a police officer, the officer was entitled to search the vehicle incident to defendant's arrest even though defendant was not an occupant of the vehicle at the time of the initial contact. [99]

- Police officers were entitled to search an automobile passenger's belongings, without probable cause to search those specific items because they had probable cause to believe that the vehicle contained contraband. [100]

- There is no such thing as *search incident to traffic citation.* [101]

- Warrantless search of an automobile can include a search of a container or package found inside the car when such a search was supported by probable cause. [102]

- The Fourth Amendment is satisfied when, under the circumstances, it is objectively reasonable for the officer to believe that the scope of the suspect's consent permitted him to open a particular container within the automobile. [103]

- The police may search an automobile and the containers within it where they have probable cause to believe contraband or evidence is contained. [104]

- Police may order persons out of an automobile during a stop for a traffic violation, and may frisk those persons for weapons if there is a reasonable belief that they are armed and dangerous. [105]

- Probable cause justifying the search of a lawfully stopped vehicle justified the search its contents that could have concealed the object of the search. [106]

POLICE TIP

When a police officer has made a lawful custodial arrest of an occupant of an automobile, the Fourth Amendment allows police to search the passenger compartment of that vehicle as a contemporaneous incident of arrest. *New York v. Belton*, 453 U.S. 454, 462 (1981)

4.3 WHEN IS IT PERMISSIBLE FOR POLICE TO SEARCH THE *PASSENGERS OF A VEHICLE?*

ANSWER

Police may search passengers of a vehicle upon their *consent.* [107] Police may also search the *belongings* of a passenger of a vehicle, if there is probable cause to believe that the vehicle contains contraband. [108]

ANALYSIS

If police have probable cause to search a lawfully stopped vehicle, they may search every part of that vehicle that may conceal the object of the search. This applies to all containers within a car regardless of whether those containers or items are owned by third parties. [109]

4.4	WHAT IS AN INVENTORY SEARCH?

ANSWER

An inventory search is an administrative procedure following the arrest of a suspect where police search and inventory a suspect's personal effects. [110]

ANALYSIS

A proper inventory search must be conducted as part of a *routine procedure* incident to incarcerating an arrested person. As part of this procedure, police may search any container or article in the suspect's possession. [111] The search is for the purpose of protecting the suspect's property. It is also to protect police from later claims by the suspect that police damaged or stole his property. This procedure should be written.

"The sanctity of private dwellings [is] ordinarily afforded the *most stringent* Fourth Amendment protection." *United States v. Martinez-Fuerte*, 428 U.S. 543, 561, (1976) (emphasis added)

Introduction

Police should almost never search a home without a warrant. Even if an exception to the warrant requirement is available, if a warrant can be obtained—obtain one. Courts jealously guard the sanctity of a person's home. Unlike most other types of searches, where the standard has increasingly become one of *reasonableness*, a house search must be authorized by a *warrant based on probable cause*. There are some exceptions to this rule, however, the court's look at these exceptions with a critical eye. The following chapter will answer questions arising from the arrest, search and seizure of persons in homes.

5.1 UNDER WHAT CIRCUMSTANCES MAY POLICE SEARCH A SUSPECT'S HOME?

ANSWER

Except for very limited exceptions, police need a search warrant to search a suspect's home. [112]

ANALYSIS

Police officers need either a *warrant or probable cause plus exigent circumstances* in order to make a lawful entry into a home. [113] A person has the highest degree of privacy protection in his home. [114] Courts are extremely reluctant to uphold the legality of warrantless searches of people's homes. Police should obtain a warrant if there is any question as to the validity of a possible warrantless entry into a residence.

 POLICE TIP

The Fourth Amendment does not protect a casual guest who is temporarily in someone else's home if that home is searched illegally. However, the Fourth Amendment does protect people if they are overnight guests in another person's home. *Minnesota v. Carter*, 525 U.S. 83, 88-89 (1998)

5.2 WHAT ARE *EXIGENT CIRCUMSTANCES* THAT WOULD JUSTIFY A WARRANTLESS ENTRY INTO A HOME?

ANSWER

A warrantless intrusion may be justified by *hot pursuit of a fleeing felon*, or *imminent destruction of evidence*, or the need to *prevent a suspect's escape*, or the *risk of danger to the police or to other persons* inside or outside the dwelling. [115]

ANALYSIS

The physical entry of the home is the chief evil against which the wording of the Fourth Amendment is directed. The main protection against improper intrusions into private homes is the requirement that police who seek to enter the home to search or arrest must first obtain a warrant. United States Supreme Court has ruled that searches and seizures inside a home without a warrant are *presumptively unreasonable.* The above exception should be used sparingly.

 POLICE TIP

Exigent circumstances exception to the warrant requirement is *not applicable* to arrest someone in his home for a *minor offense* such as a *non-jailable* traffic offense. *Welsh v. Wisconsin,* 466 U.S. 740, 750 (1984) (emphasis added)

5.3 MAY POLICE ARREST A SUSPECT IN HIS OWN HOME WITHOUT A WARRANT?

ANSWER

No.

ANALYSIS

Police may, however, arrest a suspect in *his own home* if they posses an *arrest warrant* for that suspect. For Fourth Amendment purposes, an arrest warrant founded on probable cause implicitly carries with it the limited authority to enter a dwelling in which the suspect lives when there is reason to believe the suspect is within. [116]

POLICE TIP

The Fourth Amendment permits a *protective sweep* of a person's home if the searching officer possessed a reasonable belief that the area swept harbored an individual posing a danger to the officer or others.

A "protective sweep" is a quick and limited search of premises, incident to an arrest and conducted to protect the safety of police officers or others. It is narrowly confined to a cursory visual inspection of those places in which a person might be hiding. *Maryland v. Buie*, 494 U.S. 325, 327 (1990)

5.4	DO POLICE NEED A WARRANT TO ARREST A *SUSPECT* IN A THIRD-PARTY'S HOME?

ANSWER

Yes. Police must obtain a search warrant to arrest a suspect in a third-party's home, absent exigent circumstances or consent by the homeowner. [117] Police should also have an arrest warrant.

ANALYSIS

Arrest warrants protect individuals from unreasonable seizures. Search warrants are issued upon a showing of probable cause to believe that the legitimate object of a search is located in a particular place, and therefore, safeguards an individual's privacy interest in his home against the unjustified intrusion by the police. [118] If police search a third-party's home without a warrant, they have violated the third-party's Fourth Amendment rights and not necessarily the arrestees' rights. The arrestees' rights are violated only if he can establish that he had a reasonable expectation of privacy in the third-party's home.

| 5.5 | MAY POLICE SEARCH PEOPLE *NOT THE SUBJECT OF A WARRANT* THAT HAPPEN TO BE PRESENT DURING ITS EXECUTION? |

ANSWER

No: Unless police develop an *independent safety* or *probable cause* reason.

ANALYSIS

A warrant to search a place cannot normally be construed to authorize a search of each individual in that place. [119] There may be legitimate reasons to search other individuals that are present but not subject to the warrant. If officers are arresting an individual in a home subject to an arrest warrant, they may conduct a protective sweep of the premises for officer safety. This protective sweep is a search used to find possible accomplices that may be hiding in the home. Also, if police are searching a suspect that is subject to an arrest warrant, and another person substantially interferes with the arrest, the person interfering may be arrested in his/her own right. The interfering party may now be searched incident to his/her own arrest.

5.6 MAY A *THIRD-PARTY CONSENT* TO THE SEARCH OF A PERSON'S *HOME?*

ANSWER

Yes.

ANALYSIS

The Fourth Amendment generally prohibits the warrantless entry of a person's home, whether to make an arrest or to search for specific objects. The prohibition does not apply, however, to situations in which voluntary consent has been obtained, either from the individual whose property is searched, or from a third party who possesses common authority over the premises. [120] Common authority rests on mutual use of the property by persons generally having joint access or control for most purposes." [121] However, a *physically present* co-occupant's refusal to grant consent to search a residence, under certain circumstances, will render that search invalid. [122]

 POLICE TIP

For third-party consent to be valid the third party must possess common authority or the police must reasonably believe that the person giving consent has common authority. *Illinois v. Rodriguez*, 497 U.S. 177, 186 (1990)

POLICE TIP

Courts will not invalidate a consent search if the person giving consent had apparent authority. The questions police must ask themselves are:

First – did the person in fact consent.

Second – did the person consenting to the search have the authority to consent.

Third – if it turns out that the person giving consent did not have authority, police should ask whether that person had apparent authority to give consent to search. If police reasonably believed that the person giving consent to search had authority to give consent, courts will usually uphold the search as valid.

Even when law enforcement officers have no basis for suspecting a particular individual, they may pose questions, ask for identification, and request consent to search...—provided they do not induce cooperation by coercive means. *Florida. v. Bostick*, 501 U.S. 429, 434 (1991) (emphasis added)

Introduction

If you want something—just ask. Police can make their jobs easier by simply adhering to this old adage. Asking for consent to search is one of the best tools police have at their disposal. There is nothing in the law that prevents a person from voluntarily waiving his rights. Consensual searches, like consensual statements, are just another way for a person to waive his rights. Courts do not question whether a person can give consent; rather, courts question whether consent was in fact given and if so, was it voluntary.

| 6.1 | WHAT IS A CONSENT SEARCH? |

ANSWER

Police may ask a person to *voluntarily consent* to the search of their person or property.

ANALYSIS

If a person gives *voluntary consent* to search their person or property the *Fourth Amendment does not apply*. This means, police do not need a warrant, probable cause or reasonable suspicion to conduct the search. The question courts ask is whether the consent was truly voluntary, or was it a product of express or implied *duress or coercion.* [123] Whether consent is voluntary is a question of fact to be determined from all the circumstances, and while the subject's knowledge of a right to refuse is a factor to be taken into account, the prosecution is not required to demonstrate such knowledge as a prerequisite to establishing a voluntary consent. [124] In situations where the police have some evidence of illicit activity, but lack probable cause to arrest or search, a search authorized by a valid consent may be the only means of obtaining important and reliable evidence. [125]

The following are some factors that courts consider when they are deciding if a suspect voluntarily consented: [126]

☐ Personal characteristics of the defendant, such as age, education, intelligence, sobriety, and experience with the law

☐ Context in which the consent was given, such as the length of detention or questioning, the substance of any discussion between the defendant and police preceding the consent, whether the defendant was free to leave or was subject to restraint

☐ Whether the defendant's reaction to the search was consistent with consent

☐ Court's consider suspect's age, intelligence, lack of any advice to the accused of his constitutional rights, the length of detention prior to consent, repeated and prolonged nature of the questioning [127]

In the following examples courts found that the suspect voluntarily consented to the search:

☐ Officer did not touch suspect, threaten him, display his weapon, or speak in an aggressive tone at any point during their encounter [128]

☐ If the driver has produced a valid license and proof that he is entitled to operate the car, he must be allowed to leave after the officer has issued the citation. After the initial stop has ended, further questioning by an officer is *only permissible* if the officer has a *reasonable suspicion* that the driver is engaged in illegal activity *or* the driver *voluntarily consents* to additional questioning [129]

☐ The scope of a consensual search is measured by what the reasonable person has understood by the exchange between the officer and the suspect [130]

6.2   ARE POLICE *REQUIRED* TO TELL A SUSPECT THAT THEY HAVE A RIGHT TO REFUSE TO GIVE CONSENT?

ANSWER

No.

ANALYSIS

A suspect's knowledge of his right to refuse to give consent may be *one factor* that courts consider in deciding whether the suspect gave voluntary consent. However, if the suspect is told that he has a right to refuse consent this warning will very likely be sufficient to show the court that consent was voluntarily given. [131]

6.3 MAY A *THIRD-PARTY* GIVE POLICE CONSENT TO SEARCH ANOTHER PERSON'S PROPERTY?

ANSWER

Generally.

ANALYSIS

Where two persons have equal rights to the use or occupation of premises, either may give consent to a search, and the evidence thus disclosed can be used against either. [132] Courts will permit police to search based on third-party consent even if that third-party has *less than an equal possessory interest* in the property searched. [133] Also, police are permitted to make reasonable mistakes as to the authority of the person giving consent to search. What this means is that courts generally will not invalidate a consent search if the person giving consent had *apparent authority*. (See section **5.6 Third-Party Consent**)

6.4 MAY PARENTS CONSENT TO THE SEARCH OF THEIR CHILDREN'S PROPERTY?

ANSWER

Usually.

ANALYSIS

Unless the area of the premises was *clearly and exclusively* reserved for the minor, courts generally assume that parents have control over the whole premises. This means that parents may almost always give consent to search their children's property.

6.5	WHAT ARE THE *LIMITS* OF A CONSENT SEARCH?

ANSWER

Police may only search the area that was the subject of the consent. Like all searches, consent searches must be reasonable. The courts ask: "What would the typical, reasonable person have understood by the exchange between the officer and the suspect?" [134] Just because the show of police authority might intimidate a reasonable person does not mean that all consent to searches are invalid. Courts look at all the circumstances surrounding the encounter between the police and citizen.

ANALYSIS

The following examples courts have found that the suspect did not give voluntary consent:

- It is *not voluntary* consent to the search when suspect responded "Okay" to officer's statement, "I'm going to look in here." [135]

- A state hospital implemented a policy that aimed at identifying pregnant patients suspected of drug abuse. Hospital staff members tested pregnant patients for drug abuse and reported positive tests to the police. The United States Supreme Court held that this was not voluntary consent even though the patients signed waivers. [136]

- An INS agent enticed suspect out of his apartment with a misleading story, and surprised him in the hallway with four officers instead of the single bank inspector he expected. The INS agent identified himself as an immigration officer and immediately instructed the suspect to take the agents to his apartment. The tenor of the agent's instruction was authoritative and appeared to give the suspect no option to refuse to comply. [137]

POLICE CHECKLISTS

WHAT DOES THE
FOURTH AMENDMENT REQUIRE?

☐ Do I possess a warrant based on probable cause?
[Or]
☐ Do I have an exception to the warrant and probable cause requirement?

WHEN DOES THE
FOURTH AMENDMENT APPLY?

☐ Has their been a search or seizure conducted by the police or other governmental actor?
[Or]
☐ Has there been a search or seizure made on behalf of the police or other governmental actor?

WHAT CONSTITUTES A SEARCH?

☐ Have I interfered with a suspect's reasonable expectation of privacy?

☐ Does the suspect have an actual Subjective expectation of privacy?
[And]
☐ Is the suspect's expectation of privacy likely to be viewed as objectively reasonable?

WHAT CONSTITUTES A SEIZURE OF PROPERTY?

Have I meaningfully interfered with the suspect's possessory interest in their property?

WHAT TYPES OF PROPERTY MAY I SEIZE?

- ☐ Is the property contraband?
- ☐ Is the property fruit of a crime?
- ☐ Is the property items used to commit the crime?
- ☐ Is the property the type that may be useful in proving some aspect of the crime?

WHAT ARE THE THREE TYPES OF POLICE-CITIZEN CONTACT?

- ☐ Consensual encounters: requiring no justification
- ☐ Stops: requiring reasonable suspicion
- ☐ Arrests: requiring probable cause

HOW DO I KNOW WHEN SOMEONE HAS A REASONABLE EXPECTATION OF PRIVACY?

☐ Have I interfered with the suspect's privacy in their home, which is more likely to be deemed a search, or is my interference in a place that a person has a lesser expectation of privacy, like a car?

☐ Did the suspect take steps to increase his privacy? If the suspect takes steps to ensure that his activities are kept secret (closing the window blinds or erecting a high fence on one's property) the courts are more likely to find that he has a Subjective expectation of privacy.

☐ Does my surveillance physically intrude on a suspect's property? The courts look at where a police officer is observing from, if the officer is observing a suspect's property from the street (as opposed to peering through a person's window while standing on their flower pots) the observation is less likely to be deemed a search.

☐ Have I used sophisticated technology in my surveillance? If I used technology not ordinarily available to the public, like infrared scanners, the courts' are more likely to deem my investigation a search.

> ### WHEN CAN I ARREST A SUSPECT WITHOUT A WARRANT?
>
> ☐ Do I have probable cause to believe this person committed a felony?
> ☐ Has the suspect committed a misdemeanor in my presence?
> ☐ Has the suspect committed a misdemeanor that necessitates arrest because of danger of possible injury to suspect or another person?

COURTROOM TIPS FOR POLICE
TESTIFYING IN MOTION TO SUPPRESS HEARINGS

The defense attorney is going to attempt to have the judge throw out the evidence that you worked so hard to obtain.

The following tips will help you help the State's Attorney prevent this from happening.

1. TELL THE TRUTH

The main reason to tell the truth is that it is the right thing to do. A close second is - it's the law. Lying under oath is a felony. Your credibility and reputation are more important than any individual case. Also, remember that you will be testifying in front of the same judges over and over again throughout your career. If you gain a solid reputation as an honest cop, judges will defer to your version of events in close cases.

2. EDUCATE THE STATE'S ATTORNEY BEFORE TRIAL

Give the State's Attorney information about your training and experience as a police officer. Also give the State's Attorney any related experience or education you may have in the specific area of the defendant's arrest. If the defendant was arrested for a drug crime, the State's Attorney is going to want to know about your experience as a tactical officer or undercover drug detective.

3. WRITE GOOD REPORTS

Include in your report as many facts as you can about your *pre-arrest* observations of the suspect. Defense attorneys will try to convince the judge that you did *not* have reasonable suspicion or probable cause to stop or arrest the suspect. Therefore your *pre-arrest* observations are most important at this stage. Also, remember that the defense attorney will cross-examine you regarding *specific details* contained in your report. If you do not remember a specific detail, do not speculate, guess or make one up. If you don't remember, it is okay to say that you don't remember. The State's Attorney can always refresh your memory with the police report on re-direct examination. The State's Attorney will remind the court that police reports are merely summaries of the events, and not word-for-word accounts. It is impossible for you to include in your report every relevant observation. The court will understand this.

4. **ALWAYS BE POLITE EVEN IF THE DEFENSE ATTORNEY IS NOT**

If the defense attorney acts like a jerk, that does not give you license to act in a similar manner. When the defense attorney begins to act in an unprofessional manner, it is your opportunity to draw a contrast between yourself (trustworthy professional) and the defense. If you reciprocate his boorishness with politeness—the court will perceive you as the honest professional and the defense attorney as a schoolyard bully.

5. **NEVER ARGUE WITH THE DEFENSE ATTORNEY**

Arguing with the defense attorney makes you look defensive. Let the State's Attorney make the arguments.

6. **BE PROFESSIONAL**

See above.

7. **AVOID COP-SPEAK**

If you pulled over the suspect's car—say that; don't say you *curbed his vehicle*. If the defendant was barely able to walk— say that; don't say that the defendant was not *ambulatory*. Use simple and direct words, not jargon.

Part II

WARRANTS

The primary reason for the warrant requirement is to interpose a "neutral and detached magistrate" between the citizen and "the officer engaged in the often competitive enterprise of ferreting out crime." *Johnson v. United States*, 333 U.S. 10, 14 (1948) (emphasis added)

Introduction

Part II of this book will answer some basic and essential questions about warrants. There are two primary questions that law enforcement officials must answer. First, when is a warrant required? Second, what must I include in the warrant? The answer to the first question can be a little deceiving. This is because police should sometimes get a warrant even when one is not required. That is, police should always try to obtain a warrant whenever it is practical. And whenever obtaining one does not frustrate a legitimate law enforcement purpose. Courts like warrants. The answer to the second question depends on the circumstances of the police investigation. One thing that does not change investigation-to-investigation is that every warrant must have an accompanying sworn affidavit; and every warrant must be based on probable cause and must particularly describe the place to be searched and the people or things to be seized.

7.1 WHAT IS A WARRANT AND WHEN DO POLICE NEED TO OBTAIN ONE?

ANSWER

A warrant is a document that is usually (but not exclusively) issued by a judge. It gives police authority to search or seize a person or property. The words of the Fourth Amendment require that all searches and seizures be made on the authority of a *warrant* based upon *probable cause.* Every warrant must also *particularly describe* the place to be searched and the people or things to be seized. Over the years, however, courts have created many exceptions to the warrant requirement. Now, many searches and seizures need only meet the standard of *reasonableness.*

ANALYSIS

Warrants set forth the *probable cause* for the search or seizure. Because warrants are obtained *before* any search or seizure takes place, and because a neutral person issues them, courts prefer that all searches and seizures be made on the authority of a warrant. It is not always possible for police to obtain a warrant before they search or seize persons or property. Because of this, courts have increasingly relied upon the reasonableness clause of the Fourth Amendment.

 POLICE TIP

Generally, the passage of time is the enemy of a valid warrant. Police should attempt to obtain a warrant as quickly as possible after obtaining probable cause.

POLICE TIP

Whenever possible, police should obtain a search warrant before searching a suspect's property. Police should *almost never* search a *private residence* without a search warrant or consent to search.

7.2 WHO MAY ISSUE A WARRANT?

ANSWER

Any *neutral and detached* official may approve a warrant.

ANALYSIS

The person who approves a warrant does *not* need to be a judge or even a lawyer. The only constitutional requirement is that the person approving the warrant has the ability to make an *unbiased determination* whether *probable cause* exists. [138] For all practical purposes, however, the person approving that warrant will almost always be a judge or magistrate.

POLICE TIP

The United States Supreme Court found that even a *court clerk* may issue a warrant as long as he is: *"neutral and detached." Shadwick v. Tampa*, 407 U.S. 345, 346 (1972) (Emphasis added)

7.3   WHAT ARE THE GENERAL REQUIREMENTS OF A VALID WARRANT?

ANSWER

Police must submit all warrants to a neutral and detached magistrate. All warrants must be supported by a sworn affidavit setting forth all of the facts supporting the officer's basis for probable cause. All warrants must be particular in their description of the place to be searched or the people and things to be seized.

ANALYSIS

There is no general constitutional requirement that a search warrant or arrest warrant be issued by a judge. However, this is generally the best practice because the requirement of neutrality is more easily met if a judge issues the warrant. Warrants must describe as particularly as possible the place to be searched and the people or things to be seized. Courts are very strict with this requirement. Courts are especially strict when enforcing the requirement that persons be particularly described. Police should draft an arrest warrant that leaves little room for doubt as to the person who is subject to arrest. Judges will not sign off on a warrant if there is any possibility that the wrong person might be arrested.

7.4	ARE THERE ANY SPECIAL RULES REGARDING THE EXECUTION OF A WARRANT?

ANSWER

Yes. All warrants are subject to certain limitations as to: *Time* of execution, *freshness* of probable cause, *notice* of execution, *scope* and *duration* of its execution as well as *use of force* during its execution.

ANALYSIS

In executing a warrant, law enforcement officers are limited to actions which are expressly authorized by the warrant or which are reasonably related to its purpose and are thus impliedly authorized by the warrant. [139] The following are some concrete examples of what may be authorized by a warrant either expressly or by implication:

Time of Execution

It is constitutional for police to execute a search warrant at any time—day or night—as long as the probable cause exists at the time of the warrant's execution. Police need not wait until daytime hours to execute a warrant.

Freshness of Probable Cause

All warrants have an expiration date. Because a properly drafted warrant contains good and timely probable cause, it needs to be executed while that probable cause is still fresh. Rules differ from state to state as to when the warrant expires.

A good rule of thumb is that police should attempt to execute a warrant well within 72 hours of its issuance.

Notice of its Execution

Police must generally knock-and-announce their presence and office before executing a search warrant. [140] However, the knock-and-announce requirement may give way under circumstances presenting a threat of physical violence, or where police officers have reason to believe that evidence would likely be destroyed if advance notice were given. [141]

Scope and Duration

Warrants can generally authorize the search of any location where evidence may be located and the search may be executed for any duration necessary to complete the search. The scope and duration of warrants are limited by their contents. The limits of a warrant's execution are generally contained in the warrant itself.

Use of Force in Execution

Police are generally permitted to use force in executing a search warrant. However, courts frown upon the use of excessive force. [142] The Seventh Circuit Court of Appeals refused to suppress evidence based on the following search, (however, the Court criticized police for using excessive force under the circumstances):

> "An officer pounded loudly on the door, shouting 'Decatur Police! Search warrant! Open the door!' When the occupants did not respond, the officer tried the door, found it unlocked, and opened it slightly. A second officer hit the door with a battering ram, and it flew open. One of the officers looked into the living room and, seeing no one, tossed in a concussion grenade (which the police call a "flash-bang device"). A member of the police team found Jones at a table approximately 15 to 20 feet from the front

door and instructed him to 'get down.' Instead, Jones stood up and was tackled, being struck on the right side of the neck in the process. Officers then handcuffed Jones, who had been unarmed, and conducted their search, finding marijuana, cocaine, and equipment for weighing drugs." [143]

POLICE TIP

[Federal law enforcement] A search warrant relating to offenses involving controlled substances may be served at any time of the *day or night* if the judge or United States magistrate [United States magistrate judge] issuing the warrant is satisfied that there is probable cause to believe that grounds exist for the warrant and for its service at such time. 21 USCS § 879 (2004)

7.5 MAY A WARRANT BE EXECUTED AT THE PREMISES OF SOMEONE WHO IS *NOT* A *SUSPECT?*

ANSWER

Yes.

ANALYSIS

As long as there is probable cause to believe that evidence will be found within a particular place, a warrant may be issued for the search of that place. The owner or occupant of that place being searched need not be a suspect in any crime. [144] However, additional rules may apply if the non-suspect is a journalist. [145]

POLICE TIP

Courts may issue warrants to search any property, whether or not occupied by a *third party*, where there is probable cause to believe that fruits, instrumentalities, or evidence of a crime will be found. *Zurcher v. Stanford Daily*, 436 U.S. 547, 556 (1978)

Drafting a Search Warrant: Information Sources

Obedience to the *particularity requirement* both in drafting and executing a search [or arrest] warrant is therefore essential to protect against the centuries-old fear of general searches and seizures. *United States v. Medlin*, 842 F.2d 1194, 1199 (10th Cir. 1988) (Emphasis added)

Introduction

A properly-drafted search warrant must contain specific, reliable and trustworthy information. Police may base their warrants on information derived from sources as varied as: criminal informants, private citizens, anonymous tipsters, other police or investigative agencies, or their own personal investigation or observations. You will learn in the following chapter that not all information sources are created equal.

8.1 MAY POLICE USE INFORMATION SUPPLIED BY *PRIVATE CITIZENS?*

ANSWER

Yes.

ANALYSIS

Information that is supplied to the police by ordinary citizens is *presumed to be reliable*. Ordinary citizens, who include witnesses to crimes, are not considered informants. Police may rely on their information without corroboration. Absent specific reasons for police to doubt his or her truthfulness, an ordinary citizen, who provides information to police at a crime scene or during an ongoing investigation, may be presumed credible without subsequent corroboration. [146]

8.2	MAY POLICE USE INFORMATION SUPPLIED TO THEM BY *INFORMANTS?*

ANSWER

Yes.

ANALYSIS

Information that is derived from informants must be reliable for police to use as a basis to obtain a warrant. Courts look at the totality of circumstances when they determine whether an informant's information is reliable. Courts look at factors such as the informant's truthfulness, reliability in the past, and his basis for knowing the particular information that he has given to police. [147] List this information in both the affidavit for the warrant *and* the warrant itself.

POLICE TIP

An informant's *truthfulness, reliability,* and *basis of knowledge,* are relevant in deciding whether the information he provides can be used to support a finding of probable cause. Courts, however, do not require police to provide evidence of all three. Where one of these areas is weak police may show strength in another area to make up for that deficiency. *Illinois. v. Gates*, 462 U.S. 213, 230 (1983)

POLICE TIP

Police can establish their informant's reliability by asserting in their affidavit for search warrant the following:

- Their informant has given reliable information in the past that has led to *convictions*
- (Drug investigations) They have recently used this informant for at least 3 "controlled buys"
- Asserting *very specific* information that the informant knows that would not likely be known to someone with only a casual acquaintance with the facts

---

8.3   MAY POLICE USE *HEARSAY* INFORMATION TO OBTAIN A WARRANT?

ANSWER

Yes.

ANALYSIS

Police may use hearsay information in their affidavits for warrants. Hearsay can come from citizens, informants and even from properly corroborated anonymous tips. [148] Police should always identify the source of the hearsay unless their source is an informant. If the hearsay is based on an anonymous tip, the information should be properly corroborated. This means that police must show that much of what the informant said turned out to be true. The most persuasive details to corroborate are details that only the informant would know, or that would be difficult for someone to guess. For example: Bob will leave his home at exactly 3:30 a.m., go to the trunk of his car, do a backwards flip—landing on his feet—and pull out a purple elephant-shaped bag—that bag will contain cocaine. The informant probably had inside information in this scenario; it was not likely a lucky guess.

8.4	MAY POLICE USE INFORMATION SUPPLIED BY *ANONYMOUS TIPSTERS?*

ANSWER

Yes: but only if sufficiently corroborated by the *independent observations* of police.

ANALYSIS

Anonymous tips are considered less reliable than tips from known informants, or tips from *ordinary citizens.* [149] Police are permitted to rely upon anonymous tips, if they are sufficiently corroborated by the independent observations of police. If the tip contains "not easily predicted" movements that are later corroborated, this will go a long way to show that the tip contained reliable information. [150] See above.

8.5 WHAT IS THE BEST WAY TO USE INFORMATION PROVIDED BY A *JOHN DOE* INFORMANT?

ANSWER

Whenever practical, it is best to bring *John Doe* (Anonymous) informants personally before the judge issuing the warrant.

ANALYSIS

Reviewing courts will presume that this informant is reliable. This presumption is based on the following facts:

First – the John Doe informant is generally placed under oath;

Second – the credibility and demeanor of the John Doe Informant can be personally assessed by the judge issuing the warrant;

Third – if the John Doe informant is willing to go personally before the judge, this fact alone adds to his credibility.

8.6 DO POLICE NEED TO USE AN *INFORMANT'S ACTUAL NAME* WHEN APPLYING FOR A SEARCH WARRANT?

ANSWER

No.

ANALYSIS

The Sixth Amendment of the United States Constitution provides that, "In all criminal prosecutions, the accused shall enjoy the right... to be confronted with the witnesses against him; [and] to have compulsory process for obtaining witnesses in his favor." Because the United States Supreme Court has interpreted the right to confrontation is a trial right—designed to prevent improper restrictions on the types of questions that defense counsel may ask during cross-examination—police are not constitutionally required to disclose an informant's actual name at the warrant stage of the criminal process. [151] The prosecutor will, however, have to disclose the informant's name later in the trial-process.

The Fourth Amendment states unambiguously "no Warrants shall issue, but upon probable cause, supported by Oath or affirmation, and particularly describing the place to be searched, and the persons or things to be seized." *Groh v. Ramirez*, 540 U.S. 551, 557 (2004) (Emphasis added.)

Introduction

Draft warrants very carefully. The following chapter discusses the basic building blocks of a properly drafted warrant and warrant affidavit. No two properly drafted warrants will look the same because each warrant is based on a different factual investigation. The essential elements, however, of all warrants are the same. All police should have a basic knowledge of what a properly drafted warrant looks like. This knowledge is as important to the officer executing the warrant as it is to the officer who drafted it. Why? The executing officer is responsible for the contents of the warrant he/she executes. The Fourth Amendment permits an officer to act in reasonable reliance on warrant, even if that warrant turns out to be invalid. [152] The important part of this rule, however, is that the officer's reliance must be reasonable. Therefore, learn what a properly drafted warrant looks like; the following chapter will help.

9.1 WHAT INFORMATION *MUST BE INCLUDED* IN A WARRANT?

ANSWER

Police must include the following information: the affiant (the police officer seeking the warrant), the probable cause, the source or sources of the probable cause, specific description of the place to be searched, specific description of person to be searched or seized and specific description of the things to be seized.

ANALYSIS

The Affiant:

☐ Number of years and relevant experience as a police officer
☐ Number of years investigating the type of crime in question
☐ Number of this specific type of investigation (drug buys)
☐ Any unique training received that applies to the type of investigation being done

The Probable Cause:

☐ Include specific information suggesting evidence of a crime will be located at the place described
☐ Include specific information suggesting that a specific person committed a crime (arrest warrant)
☐ Remember that courts look at the evidence as a whole, not each specific section of the warrant
☐ Include preliminary matches of prints and DNA if available
☐ Include information that would not necessarily be admitted at trial

The Source or Sources of Probable Cause:

☐ Include information from ordinary citizens or witnesses, if available and they are presumed reliable

☐ Include information about informant's past reliability (past information given led to convictions)

☐ Include information about informant's past reliability generally

☐ Establish reliability with controlled buys (at least 3 buys for a drug case)

☐ Use hearsay information but show its reliability

☐ Use information from anonymous tips but corroborate this information

Specific Description of Place to be Searched:

☐ Leave no room for guessing as to the place to be searched

☐ Use specific address for home (123 Fake Street, Chicago, IL 60148)

☐ Use specific apartment number for apartment (123 Fake Street, Apt. 101, Chicago, IL 60148)

☐ There must be no question as to the exact location of the place to be searched

---

9.2 WHAT INFORMATION OUGHT TO BE *LEFT OUT* OF A WARRANT?

ANSWER

Any Information that is not necessary to establish the factors listed in 9.1.

ANALYSIS

Do not get the wrong idea, police need to draft warrants with plenty of specific details. In fact, if the warrant is drafted too generally a court will likely find it to be insufficient or entirely invalid. However, warrants need not include exact amounts of drugs to be found, exact times of execution or the exact times of the previous controlled buys. This type of information is not necessary and will only give a defense attorney material to draw from for cross-examination.

9.3   HOW *SPECIFIC* MUST A WARRANT BE IN DESCRIBING THE *THINGS TO BE SEIZED?*

ANSWER

A search warrant must be *very specific* as to the things police intend to seize.

ANALYSIS

If police intend to seize guns they should recite in their warrant the type of guns they expect to find (although serial numbers are not required). If police intend to seize drugs they should recite the types of drugs they expect to find (although exact amount is not required). Police may include "mere evidence" language, that is, language that covers all other evidence of crime. However, courts may deem this language too general, so police should make sure this language is coupled with other, very specific language.

POLICE TIP

It is important for police to remember that the warrant itself must contain specific language. It is not sufficient that the affidavit or application contain specific language if the warrant does not also have that language. *Groh v. Ramirez*, 540 U.S. 551, 554-557 (2004)

9.4   HOW *SPECIFIC* MUST A WARRANT BE IN *DESCRIBING THE PLACE TO BE SEARCHED?*

ANSWER

The warrant should be drafted so specifically as to leave no doubt as to the exact location of the place to be searched. If the

 POLICE TIP

Make sure that the entire warrant is drafted with care. If a reviewing court determines that: "a search warrant affidavit contains a false, material statement made intentionally or with reckless disregard for the truth, the reviewing court must excise the offensive language from the affidavit and determine whether the remaining portion establishes probable cause." See, *Franks v. Delaware*, 438 U.S. 154, (1978) (emphasis added)

warrant is ambiguous as to the location to be searched, a court could invalidate the entire warrant.

ANALYSIS

The Warrant Clause of the Fourth Amendment categorically prohibits the issuance of any warrant except one "particularly describing the place to be searched and the persons or things to be seized." The purpose of the particularity requirement was to prevent general searches. By limiting the authorization to search to the specific areas and things for which there is probable cause to search, the requirement ensures that the search will be carefully tailored to its justifications, and will not take on the character of the wide-ranging exploratory searches the Framers intended to prohibit. [153]

Chapter 10

Post Arrest Investigation

A suspect must be told that he has the right to remain silent, that anything he says can be used against him in a court of law, that he has the right to the presence of an attorney during questioning, and that if he cannot afford an attorney one will be appointed for him prior to any questioning. *Miranda v. Arizona*, 384 U.S. 436, 471 (1966)

Introduction

The most important part of the post-arrest investigation is the police interview of the suspect. Police responsibility to provide a suspect his Miranda warnings is probably the most known but least understood responsibility of law enforcement. Many in the public don't understand, and police sometimes forget, that police are required to apprise a suspect of his Miranda rights only under a certain set of circumstances—not in every case. What law requires and what is prudent police practice can be two different things. The following chapter will answer some important questions regarding the post arrest investigation with a particular focus on the interview of the suspect.

10.1 WHEN MUST POLICE GIVE A SUSPECT HIS MIRANDA WARNINGS?

ANSWER

Police are required to give a suspect his Miranda rights only after the suspect is in custody, but before he is questioned. In

83

short, the suspect must be subject to custodial interrogation for Miranda to apply.

ANALYSIS

Custodial interrogation means questioning initiated by law enforcement officers after a person has been taken into custody or otherwise deprived of his freedom of action in any significant way. [154] If the suspect is free to leave during the questioning, police are not required to give him Miranda warnings. Also, if a suspect is in custody—and without any questioning or prompting by police—he decides to make a voluntary statement, that statement will be admissible in court even if police did not give that suspect the Miranda warnings.

10.2   UNDER WHAT CIRCUMSTANCES MAY A SUSPECT WAIVE HIS MIRANDA RIGHTS?

ANSWER

A suspect may waive his Miranda rights and speak with police at any time. But the suspect's waiver of his Miranda rights must be *knowing and intelligent.*

ANALYSIS

"The constitutional minimum for determining whether a waiver was 'knowing and intelligent' is that the accused be made sufficiently aware of his right to have counsel present and of the possible consequences of a decision to forgo the aid of counsel." [155] This standard is the same whether the suspect is waiving his Sixth Amendment or Fifth Amendment right to counsel. [156]

10.3 DOES A SUSPECT'S MIRANDA WAIVER HAVE TO BE IN WRITING TO BE VALID?

ANSWER

No.

ANALYSIS

Miranda Waivers need only be knowing and intelligent to be valid. There is no requirement that they be in writing. Police ought to have a suspect sign a written waiver as a matter of good police practice. "An expressly written or oral statement of waiver of the right to remain silent, or of the right to counsel, is usually strong proof of the validity of that waiver, but is not inevitably either necessary or sufficient to establish waiver. The question is not one of form, but rather whether the defendant in fact knowingly and voluntarily waived the rights delineated in the Miranda case." [157]

10.4 ARE POLICE *REQUIRED* TO PROVIDE A SUSPECT AN ATTORNEY IF HE ASKS, "DO YOU THINK I NEED A LAWYER?"

ANSWER

No. (Maybe?)

ANALYSIS/ EXAMPLES:

Police do not have to stop questioning if a suspect makes a reference to an attorney that is *ambiguous* or *equivocal*, in that a reasonable officer in light of the circumstances would have understood only that the suspect might be invoking the right to counsel. [158] However, a suspect who has invoked the right to counsel cannot be questioned regarding any offense unless an attorney is actually present. [159] Once an individual in custody invokes his right to counsel, interrogation must cease until an attorney is present; at that point, the individual must have an opportunity to confer with the attorney and to have him present during any subsequent questioning. [160]

10.5   MAY POLICE QUESTION A SUSPECT ABOUT A CRIME IF HE IS *IN CUSTODY FOR ANOTHER CRIME?*

ANSWER

Yes, if the suspect waives his Fifth Amendment Miranda rights.

ANALYSIS/EXAMPLES:

Police need to be careful not to confuse a suspect's Fifth Amendment privilege against self-incrimination with a suspect's Sixth Amendment right to counsel. A suspect's Sixth Amendment right to counsel is triggered at the time the state initiates adversary judicial proceedings against the suspect; adversary judicial proceedings can be initiated by way of formal charge, preliminary hearing, indictment, information, or arraignment. [161] The Sixth Amendment right to counsel is "offense specific." [162] This means that if the defendant is charged with one crime, police are not automatically precluded from questioning the defendant about a different crime. However, the regular Fifth Amendment rules do apply.

POLICE TIP

If a suspect indicates that he wishes to be *silent* after being read his Miranda rights, police must honor that request. If, however, the suspect unequivocally requests an attorney, he may not be questioned again until his attorney is present, or until he reinitiates dialog with police.

10.6   DO POLICE HAVE TO PROVIDE A SUSPECT AN ATTORNEY FOR A LINE-UP?

ANSWER

No.

ANALYSIS

Suspects do not have a right to the presence of an attorney during a line-up or show-up, as long as they take place before the defendant is formally charged. [163] The United States Supreme Court has defined formal charge as any of the following: preliminary hearing, indictment, information, or arraignment. [164]

10.7 IS IT PERMISSIBLE FOR POLICE TO *LIE* TO A SUSPECT TO GAIN HIS CONFESSION?

ANSWER

Yes.

ANALYSIS/EXAMPLES:

Any statement given freely and voluntarily is admissible in evidence. Ploys to mislead a suspect or lull him into a false sense of security are permissible as long as they do not rise to the level of compulsion or coercion. [165] Police must be careful that they do not go too far. State's Attorneys, however, are not permitted to lie to suspects.

Table of Authorities

[1] *Katz v. United States*, 389 U.S. 347, 351 (1967) (emphasis added)

[2] *United States v. Jacobsen*, 466 U.S. 109, 113 (1984) (emphasis added)

[3] *Mapp v. Ohio*, 367 U.S. 643, 655 (1961) (emphasis added)

[4] *Illinois v. Caballes*, 2005 U.S. LEXIS 769, (January 24, 2005) (not yet published in final version)

[5] *United States v. Fulani*, 277 F. Supp. 2d 454 (2003)

[6] *United States v. Duong*, 336 F. Supp, 2d 967 (2004)

[7] *United States v. Burbage*, 365 F.3d 1174 (2004) (emphasis added)

[8] *Shaul v. Cherry Valley-Springfield Cent. Sch. Dist.*, 218 F.Supp. 2d 266 (2002)

[9] *United States v. Lonedog*, 67 Fed. Appx. 543 (10th Cir., 2003)

[10] *United States v. Flynn*, 309 F.3d 736 (10th Cir., 2002)

[11] *United States v. Fulani*, 368 F.3d 351 (3rd Cir., 2004)

[12] *United States v. Payne*, 99 Fed. Appx. 204 (10th Cir., 2004)

[13] *Katz v. United States*, 389 U.S. 347, 351 (1967) (emphasis added)

[14] *Katz v. United States*, 389 U.S. 347, 351 (1967)

[15] *Illinois v. Andreas*, 463 U.S. 765 (1983)

[16] *United States v. Place*, 462 U.S. 696 (1983)

[17] *United States v. Williams*, 902 F.2d 678 (8th Cir., 1990)

[18] *Reynolds v. United States*, 449 U.S. 954 (1980) (emphasis added)

[19] *United States v. Gunn*, 428 F.2d 1057 (5th Cir., 1970)

[20] *Fla. v. Riley*, 488 U.S. 445 (1989)

[21] *United States v. Place*, 462 U.S. 696, 707 (1983)

[22] *United States v. Jacobsen*, 466 U.S. 109, 113 (1984) (emphasis added)

[23] *INS v. Delgado*, 466 U.S. 210 (1984) (emphasis added)

[24] *United States v. Drayton*, 536 U.S. 194 (2002)

[25] *Terry v. Ohio*, 392 U.S. 1, 31 (1968)

[26] *United States v. Taylor*, 956 F.2d 572, 577 (6th Cir. 1992)

[27] *Florida v. Bostick*, 501 U.S. 429 at 434-435 (1991)

[28] *Ohio v. Robinette*, 519 U.S. 33, 40 (1996)

[29] *New York v. Class*, 475 U.S. 106, 114 (1986)

[30] *State v. Gahner*, 554 N.W.2d 818, 820 (N.D. S.Ct. 1996)

[31] *People v. Melton*, 910 P.2d 672, 676 (Colo. S.Ct. 1996)

[32] *Terry v. Ohio*, 392 U.S. 1 (1968) (emphasis added)

[33] *United States v. Mendenhall*, 446 U.S. 544, 554 (1980) (emphasis added)

[34] *Terry v. Ohio*, 392 U.S. 1, 9 (1968) (emphasis added)

[35] *Terry v. Ohio*, 392 U.S. 1 at 30 (1968) (emphasis added)

[36] *United States v. Cortez*, 449 U.S. 411, 417 (1981) (emphasis added)

[37] *Terry v. Ohio*, 392 U.S. 1, 20 (1968) (emphasis added)

[38] *United States v. Mendenhall*, 446 U.S. 544 (1980) (emphasis added)

[39] *California v. Hodari D.*, 499 U.S. 621 (1991)

[40] *California v. Hodari D.*, 499 U.S. 621, 626 (1991) (emphasis added)

[41] *United States v. Cortez*, 449 U.S. 411, 417-418 (1981) (emphasis added)

[42] *Adams v. Williams*, 407 U.S. 143, 146 (1972)

[43] *Ornelas v. United States*, 517 U.S. 690, 695 (1996)

[44] *United States v. Sokolow*, 490 U.S. 1, 7 (1989) (emphasis added)

[45] *Adams v. Williams*, 407 U.S. 143, 145 (1972)

[46] *Ill. v. Wardlow*, 528 U.S. 119, 126 (2000) (emphasis added)

[47] *Ornelas v. United States*, 517 U.S. 690, 696 (1996) (emphasis added)

[48] *Illinois. v. Wardlow*, 528 U.S. 119, 124 (2000)

[49] *Illinois. v. Wardlow*, 528 U.S. 119, 124 (2000)

[50] *United States v. Brignoini-Ponce*, 422 U.S. 873, 885 (1975)

[51] *United States v. Montoya De Hernandez*, 473 U.S. 531, 542 (1985)

[52] *Terry v. Ohio*, 392 U.S. 1, at 5-6 (1968) (emphasis added)

[53] *United States v. Ortiz*, 422 U.S. 891, 897 (1975) (emphasis added)

[54] *United States v. Brown*, 159 F.3d 147,150 (3rd Cir. 1998)

[55] *Terry v. Ohio*, 392 U.S. 1, 30 (1968) (emphasis added)

[56] *Minnesota v. Dickerson*, 508 U.S. 366, 378 (1993) (emphasis added)

[57] *United States v. Stanfield*, 109 F.3d 976, 984 (4th Cir. 1997)

[58] *United States v. Harris*, 313 F.3d 1228, 1236 (10th Cir. 2002) (emphasis added)

[59] *United States v. Mireles*, 583 F.2d 1115, 1116 (10th Cir. 1978)

[60] *United States v. Michelletti*, 13 F.3d 838, 842 (5th Cir. 1994)

[61] *United States v. Proctor*, 148 F.3d 39, 42 (1st Cir. 1998)

[62] *United States v. Proctor*, 148 F.3d 39, 42 (1st Cir. 1998)

[63] *Pennsylvania v. Mimms*, 434 U.S. 106 (5th Cir. 1994)

[64] *Maryland v. Wilson*, 519 U.S. 408, 414 (1997)

[65] *Michigan v. Long*, 463 U.S. 1032, 1045-1046 (1983)

[66] *United States v. Miles*, 247 F.3d 1009 (9th Cir. 2001) (emphasis added)

[67] *Washington v. Lambert*, 98 F.3d 1181, 1185 (9th Cir., 1996)

[68] *Florida v. Royer*, 460 U.S. 491 (1983)

[69] *Dunaway v. New York*, 442 U.S. 200 (1979)

[70] *United States v. Thompson*, 906 F.2d 1292 (8th Cir.1990)

[71] *Washington v. Lambert*, 98 F.3d 1181, 1187 (9th Cir. 1996) (emphasis added)

[72] *United States v. Bravo*, 295 F.3d 1002 (9th Cir., 2002)

[73] *United States v. Jones*, 759 F.2d 633, 637 (8th Cir., 1985)

[74] *California v. Hodari D.*, 499 U.S. 621, 628-629 (1991) (emphasis added)

[75] *United States v. Watson*, 423 U.S. 411, 424 (1976) (emphasis added)

[76] *United States v. Watson*, 423 U.S. 411, 422 (1976) (emphasis added)

[77] *Briegar v. United States*, 338 U.S. 160, 175-176 (1949) (emphasis added)

[78] *Illinois. v. Gates*, 462 U.S. 213 (1983) (emphasis added)

[79] *Maryland v. Pringle*, 540 U.S. 366 (2003) (emphasis added)

[80] *United States v. Arvizu*, 534 U.S. 266, 274 (2002) (emphasis added)

[81] *United States v United States v. Bonner*, 363 F.3d 213 (3rd Cir., 2004) (emphasis added) *Illinois. Arvizu*, 534 U.S. 266, 274 (2002) (emphasis added)

[82] *Hill v. California*, 401 U.S. 797, 803 (1971) (emphasis added)

[83] *United States v. Arvizu*, 534 U.S. 266, 273 (2002) (emphasis added)

[84] *United States v. Mayo*, 394 F.3d 1271 (9th Cir. 2005) (emphasis added)

[85] *Illinois. v. Wardlow*, 528 U.S. 119, 124 (2000) (emphasis added)

[86] *United States v. $242,484.00 United States Currency*, 389 F.3d 1149 (11th Cir. 2004) (emphasis added)

87 *Illinois. v. Wardlow*, 528 U.S. 119, 124 (2000) (emphasis added)

88 *Illinois. v. Gates*, 462 U.S. 213, 230 (1983)

89 *Alabama. v. White*, 496 U.S. 325, 326 (1990)

90 *Illinois. v. Gates*, 462 U.S. 213, 230 (1983) (emphasis added)

91 *Illinois. v. Gates*, 462 U.S. 213, 241 (1983)

92 *Florida. v. J.L.*, 529 U.S. 266,270 (2000)

93 *United States v. Robinson*, 414 U.S. 218 (1973) (emphasis added)

94 *New York v. Belton*, 453 U.S. 454 (1981)

95 *Chambers v. Maroney*, 399 U.S. 42 (1970) (emphasis added)

96 *United States v. Edwards*, 415 U.S. 800 (1974)

97 *Pennsylvania v. Labron*, 518 U.S. 938, 940 (1996) (emphasis added)

98 *New York v. Belton*, 453 U.S. 454 (1981) (emphasis added)

99 *Thornton v. United States*, 541 U.S. 615 (2004)

100 *Wyo. v. Houghton*, 526 U.S. 295, 302 (1999)

101 *Knowles v. Iowa*, 525 U.S. 113, 119 (1998) (emphasis added)

102 *United States v. Ross*, 456 U.S. 798 (1982)

103 *Florida v. Jimeno*, 500 U.S. 248, 249 (1991)

104 *California v. Acevedo*, 500 U.S. 565, 580 (1991)

105 *Pennsylvania v. Mimms*, 434 U.S. 106, 111 (1977)

106 *United States v. Ross*, 456 U.S. 798 (1982)

107 *United States v. Drayton*, 536 U.S. 194, 197 (2002) (emphasis added)

108 *Wyoming. v. Houghton*, 526 U.S. 295, 302 (1999)

109 *Wyoming. v. Houghton*, 526 U.S. 295, 302-303 (1999)

110 *Illinois v. Lafayette*, 462 U.S. 640, 644 (1983)

111 *Illinois v. Lafayette*, 462 U.S. 640, 648 (1983) (emphasis added)

112 *Steagald v.United States*, 451 U.S. 204, 211 (1981) (emphasis added)

113 *Kirk v. Louisiana*, 536 U.S. 635, 638 (2002) (emphasis added)

114 *Welsh v. Wisconsin*, 466 U.S. 740, 748 (1984)

115 *Minnesota v. Olson*, 495 U.S. 91, 97 (1990) (emphasis added)

116 *Payton v. New York*, 445 U.S. 573 (1980)

117 *Steagald v. United States*, 451 U.S. 204, 205 (1981) (emphasis added)

118 *Steagald v. United States*, 451 U.S. 204, 213 (1981) (emphasis added)

Table of Authorities

[119] *Ybarra v. Illinois*, 444 U.S. 85 (1979)

[120] *Illinois v. Rodriguez*, 497 U.S. 177, 179 (1990) (emphasis added)

[121] *Illinois v. Rodriguez*, 497 U.S. 177, 181 (1990) (emphasis added)

[122] *Georgia v. Randolph* U.S. Supreme Court No. 04-1067 (decided March 22, 2006)

[123] *Schneckloth v. Bustamonte*, 412 U.S. 218, 248 (1973) (emphasis added)

[124] *Schneckloth v. Bustamonte*, 412 U.S. 218, 248 (1973)

[125] *Schneckloth v. Bustamonte*, 412 U.S. 218, 248 (1973)

[126] *United States v. Welerford*, 356 F.3d 932, 936 (8th Cir. 2004)

[127] *United States v. Mancias*, 350 F.3d 800, 804-805 (8th Cir. 2003)

[128] *United States v. Rosborough*, 366 F.3d 1145, 1149 (10th Cir. 2004)

[129] *United States v. Taverna*, 348 F.3d 873, 878 (10th Cir. 2003) (emphasis added)

[130] *Florida v. Jimeno*, 500 U.S. 248, 251 (1991)

[131] *Schneckloth v. Bustamonte*, 412 U.S. 218, 248 (1973)

[132] *United States v. Sferas*, 210 F.2d 69 (7th Cir. 1954)

[133] *Frazier v. Cupp*, 394 U.S. 731 (1969) (emphasis added)

[134] *Florida v. Jimeno*, 500 U.S. 248, 251 (1991) (emphasis added)

[135] *United States v. Weidul*, 325 F.3d 50, 53 (1st Cir. 2003) (emphasis added)

[136] *Ferguson v. City of Charleston*, 532 U.S. 67, 86 (2001)

[137] *Orhorhaghe v. INS*, 38 F.3d 488, 496 (9th Cir. 1994)

[138] *Shadwick v. Tampa*, 407 U.S. 345, 346 (1972) (emphasis added)

[139] *Michigan v. Summers*, 452 U.S. 692, 705 (1981)

[140] *Wilson v. Arkansas*, 514 U.S. 927 (1995)

[141] *Richards v. Wisconsin*, 520 U.S. 385 (1997) (emphasis added)

[142] *United States v. Jones*, 214 F.3d 836, 837 (7th Cir. 2000)

[143] *United States v. Jones*, 214 F.3d 836, 837 (7th Cir. 2000)

[144] *Zurcher v. Stanford Daily*, 436 U.S. 547, 549-550 (1978)

[145] 42 USCS § 2000aa (2004) (emphasis added)

[146] *United States v. Blount*, 123 F.3d 831, 835 (5th Cir. 1997)

[147] *Illinois. v. Gates*, 462 U.S. 213, 230 (1983) (emphasis added)

[148] *Illinois. v. Gates*, 462 U.S. 213, 232-235 (1983) (emphasis added)

[149] *Florida. v. J.L.*, 529 U.S. 266, 269 (2000) (emphasis added)

[150] *Florida. v. J.L.*, 529 U.S. 266, 269 (2000)

[151] *Pennsylvania v. Ritchie*, 480 U.S. 39, 52 (1987) (emphasis added)

[152] *United States v. Leon*, 468 U.S. 897, 920, (1984) (emphasis added)

[153] *Maryland v. Garrison*, 480 U.S. 79, 84 (1987) (emphasis added)

[154] *Miranda v. Arizona*, 384 U.S. 436, 444 (1966) (emphasis added)

[155] *Patterson v. Illinois*, 487 U.S. 285, 292 (1988)

[156] *Patterson v. Illinois*, 487 U.S. 285, 292 (1988)

[157] *North Carolina v. Butler*, 441 U.S. 369, 373 (1979) (emphasis added)

[158] *Davis v. United States*, 512 U.S. 452, 459 (1994) (emphasis added)

[159] *Edwards v. Arizona*, 451 U.S. 477, 484-485 (1981) (emphasis added)

[160] *Minnick v. Mississippi*, 498 U.S. 146, 152-156 (1990)

[161] *Brewer v. Williams*, 430 U.S. 387, 398 (1977) (emphasis added)

[162] *Texas. v. Cobb*, 532 U.S. 162, 164 (2001)

[163] *Kirby v. Illinois*, 406 U.S. 682, 690 (1972)

[164] *Brewer v. Williams*, 430 U.S. 387, 398 (1977)

[165] *Illinois. v. Perkins*, 496 U.S. 292, 297 (1990) (emphasis added)

Index

Abandoned 5
Abandoned property 6
Abandonment 6
Anonymous tips 31
Anonymous tipsters 71
Apparent authority 47, 52
Armed and dangerous 22
Arrest 14
Arrest warrant 27
Arrest-power rule 25
Automatic right to search 22
Automobile 16, 33
Brief investigatory stops 17
Canine 9
Check for weapons 23
Common authority 46
Consensual encounter 14
Consent 19
Consent search 47
Consent to search 10
Container or package 37
Containers within a car 38
Contraband 7
Cop-speak 59
Criminal informants 71
Cusory visual inspection 44
Custodial interrogation 84
Defense attorney 58
Destruction of evidence 42
Dog sniff 9
Dog sniffs 5
Driver's license 16
Drug checkpoint 7
Drug investigations 73
Duress or coercion 50
Eavesdropping 9
Eavesdropping 9

Evasive behavior 20
Evidence; primary forms of ii
Exclusionary rule 3, 9
Exigent circumstances 41
Extended questioning 18
Felony 26
Fourth Amendment 3, 9, 64
Frisk 23
Frisk for weapons 22
Furtive actions 20
General searches 82
Governmental actor 4
Hearsay 73
Hearsay informants 31
High crime area 20
High drug crime area 31
Home 25
Hot pursuit 42
Identification 19
Informants 30, 72
Infrared scanners 56
INS 53
Inventory search 39
Investigatory stop 14
John Doe (Anonymous) informants 75
Journalist 69
Knock-and-announce 68
Limited search 36
Line-up 87
Meaningful interference 10
Mere evidence 7, 80
Minor traffic offenses 36
Miranda Waivers 85
Miranda warnings 84
Misdemeanor 26, 27
Motion to suppress hearings 58
Motor vehicle 9
Ordinary citizens 74
Overnight guests 42

Passenger compartment of a vehicle 36
Passengers 23
Physical evidence ii
Physical force 17, 26
Plain view doctrine 5
Possessory interest in property 3
Private citizens 71
Private individuals 5
Probable cause 14, 17, 24
Protective sweep 44
Public airways 9
Public arrests 25
Public place 15, 17
Public places 25
Public view 5
Reasonable expectation of privacy 5, 6
Reasonable mistakes by police 30
Reasonable person standard 15
Reasonable suspicion 14
Search 3
     defined 8
Search incident to arrest 32
Search warrant 27
Security guards 4
Seizure 3
Seizure of persons 15
Seizure of property 10
Show of authority 18, 26
Show-up 87
Sixth Amendment 86
Statements; gathering ii
Subjective expectation of privacy 56
Surveillance 56
Suspects ii
Suspect's home 41
Suspicious behavior 29
Terry stop 14
Third parties 38
Third-party consent 46

Third-party's home 44
Threatening language 18
Totality of the circumstances 6, 17, 19
Traffic violation 37
United States v. Katz 8
Unprovoked flight 20
Unreasonable searches 5
Use of force 67
Vehicle searches 35
Violent crime 24
Voluntary consent 5, 49
Warrant 10
Warrant affidavit 77
Warrantless arrests 25
Warrantless seizure 7
Weapons 21

NOTES

NOTES

NOTES

NOTES

Suicide by Cop
*Practical Direction for Recognition, Resolution
    and Recovery*
by Vivian Lord

Police Sergeant Examination Preparation Guide
by Larry Jetmore

Path of the Warrior
*An Ethical Guide to Personal & Professional
    Development in the Field of Criminal
    Justice*
by Larry F. Jetmore

The COMPSTAT Paradigm
*Management Accountability in Policing,
    Business and the Public Sector*
by Vincent E. Henry, CPP, Ph.D.

The New Age of Police Supervision and Management
A Behavioral Concept
by Michael A. Petrillo & Daniel R. DelBagno

Effective Police Leadership - 2nd Edition
Moving Beyond Management
by Thomas E. Baker, Lt. Col. MP USAR (Ret.)

The Lou Savelli Pocketguides -

Gangs Across America and Their Symbols
Identity Theft - *Understanding and Investigation*
Guide for the War on Terror
Basic Crime Scene Investigation
Spanish for Law Enforcement Officers
Graffiti
Street Drugs
Cop Jokes

(800) 647-5547   www.LooseleafLaw.com